Fusion
of the
Eight Psychic
Channels

Fusion
of the
Eight Psychic Channels

Opening and Sealing the
Energy Body

Mantak Chia

Destiny Books
Rochester, Vermont

Destiny Books
One Park Street
Rochester, Vermont 05767
www.DestinyBooks.com

Destiny Books is a division of Inner Traditions International

Originally published in Thailand in 2006 by Universal Tao Publications under the title *Fusion of the Eight Psychic Channels: Opening and Sealing Psychic Channels*

Library of Congress Cataloging-in-Publication Data
Chia, Mantak, 1944–
  Fusion of the eight psychic channels : opening and sealing the energy body / Mantak Chia.
    p. cm.
  Includes bibliographical references and index.
  ISBN 978-1-59477-138-5 (pbk.)
  1. Hygiene, Taoist. 2. Philosophy, Taoist. I. Title.
  RA781.C4875 2008
  613—dc22
                                                              2008030762

Printed and bound in India by Gopsons Papers, Ltd.

10 9 8 7 6 5 4 3 2 1

Text design and layout by Jon Desautels
This book was typeset in Janson

 Contents

Acknowledgments

We extend our gratitude to the many generations of Taoist masters who have passed on their special lineage, in the form of an unbroken oral transmission, over thousands of years. We wish to especially thank Taoist Master Yi Eng for his patience and openness in transmitting the formulas of Taoist Inner Alchemy. We also wish to thank the thousands of unknown men and women of the Chinese healing arts who developed many of the methods and ideas presented in this book.

We offer our eternal gratitude to our parents and teachers for their many gifts to us. Remembering them brings joy and satisfaction to our continued efforts in presenting the Universal Tao System. As always, their contribution has been crucial in presenting the concepts and techniques of the Universal Tao.

We thank the many contributors essential to this book's final form: The editorial and production staff at Inner Traditions/Destiny Books for their efforts to clarify the text and produce a handsome new edition of the book, Nancy Yeilding for her line edit of the new edition, and the artist, Juan Li, for the use of his beautiful and visionary paintings and drawings, illustrating Taoist esoteric practices.

We wish to thank the following people for their assistance in producing the original edition of this book: Lee J. Holden Jr. and Angela Dawn Babcock for their writing and editorial contributions, Udon for his illustrations, book layout, and beautiful cover, Wilbert Wils and Jean Chilton for their assistance in preparing, editing, and proofreading the manuscript, and Jettaya Phaobtong and Saumya

Comer for their editorial contributions to the revised edition.

A special thank you goes to our Thai Production Team: Raruen Keawpadung, computer graphics; Saysunee Yongyod, photographer; Udon Jandee, illustrator; and Saniem Chaisarn, production designer.

Putting Fusion of the Eight Psychic Channels into Practice

The practices described in this book have been used successfully for thousands of years by Taoists trained by personal instruction. Readers should not undertake the practice without receiving personal transmission and training from a certified instructor of the Universal Tao, since certain of these practices, if done improperly, may cause injury or result in health problems. This book is intended to supplement individual training by the Universal Tao and to serve as a reference guide for these practices. Anyone who undertakes these practices on the basis of this book alone, does so entirely at his or her own risk.

The meditations, practices, and techniques described herein are *not* intended to be used as an alternative or substitute for professional medical treatment and care. If any readers are suffering from illnesses based on mental or emotional disorders, an appropriate professional health care practitioner or therapist should be consulted. Such problems should be corrected before you start training.

This book does not attempt to give any medical diagnosis, treatment, prescription, or remedial recommendation in relation to any human disease, ailment, suffering, or physical condition whatsoever.

The Universal Tao and its staff and instructors cannot be responsible for the consequences of any practice or misuse of the information contained in this book. If the reader undertakes any exercise without strictly following the instructions, notes, and warnings, the responsibility must lie solely with the reader.

Understanding
the Tao

The Fusion of the Eight Psychic Channels practice forms the final aspect of the group of Universal Tao practices known as Inner Alchemy. It builds upon the practices found in *Fusion of the Five Elements* and *Cosmic Fusion*. All of the fusion practices focus on clearing the various energy pathways in the body and are prerequisites for the practice of the Immortal Tao, found in *The Taoist Soul Body*. The opening of the psychic channels enables practitioners to balance and regulate the energy flow throughout the body and to offer healing energy to Earth as well.

FROM THE CONDITIONED MIND
TO TAOISM

Studying the Tao is like discovering that your inner world is as vast as outer space, and exploring that space with new cameras, telescopes, and satellites. Or it is like investigating the deepest abyss of the ocean in a submarine. It is a process of opening up to a body of infinite space.

When you open your body you open your mind as well; more specifically, you open what some call the third eye, a sense organ

Fig. 1.1. Communicate with expanding creation.

capable of sensing innumerable dimensions and possibilities. This is something that will release you from what you know as life, with its repetitious work or school, week after week, year after year. It has this possibility because within the mind there is no experience other than that of expanding creation or Wu Chi (Nothingness) (fig. 1.1).

To truly see this expanding creation is to see it as an actual "object" that you can hold and work with. The energy of creation can be very strong or less intense; it is a choice you make. It can be put into your heart, eyes, or thoughts. It is a very strong healing force, because it is the essence of creation, which is something far beyond the limits of your conditioned mind. Opening your mind enables this energy to expand. Then your natural healing energy, love, and creative energy can create something beautiful within your being (fig. 1.2).

Fig. 1.2. Did you know you can reach a natural continuous state of bliss?

Change into the Light

Like many other people, you may sometimes feel like you have no power and cannot change anything. This is actually the essence of depression: the feeling of being trapped. The feeling that you cannot change your family or the world may lead to sadness, a sense of confinement, and stagnation. But you can. In fact it is simple, once you acknowledge that the world is constantly changing and learn how to join your energy to that. As you increase your energy with love and happiness, you will enter the fresh beautiful river of change and creation.

You see, all negative thoughts serve to limit the mind. They make the mind its own slave. Negative thoughts pull your mind away from the river of creation. For example, after watching a horror movie you may find it difficult to go into the forest by yourself because you are fearful of bad things that might be creeping in the woods. But if you did not watch that horror movie and instead meditated using your third eye, you could serenely go into the forest and stare at the full moon (fig. 1.3). After falling in love with the moon you could go home to your family and spoon-feed them with the creation energy you acquired from the moonlit forest.

If we act like we know everything life becomes boring and stagnated. But if we understand that the energy of creation is infinite, then we can see that life holds boundless glory outside the limits of our conditioned minds. This glory makes life wonderfully beautiful to

Fig. 1.3. The full moon's energy inspires your true self to awaken.

live. It is only our negative thoughts that keep our mind confined to a limited posture of living.

Creation energy or chi energy is the single basic element of all things in existence. It created everything and will create everything that will ever exist. The teachings of the Tao offer a way to explore this energy, to connect with it mentally and physically, and to let it open a new vision of life, freeing our conditioned minds that prevent us from finding a life of unlimited potential.

Creating Treasure

The Tao is so beautiful because you can "open" to it at any age, and feel like you have just discovered a treasure. When this feeling winds through your body, you look for further treasures, which you will find at each point in your body that is healed by being saturated with chi (life-force energy). Gradually your whole body will come to glow like a rare treasure.

Although you cannot take your diamonds or gold with you when you die, you can take this treasure of a magnetic compassionate heart. So do not sell yourself short; start opening up the pathways and channels of your body and send the chi through them. The sensation can get as strong as you allow, to heal your broken heart, toxic-ridden liver, and lungs, or whatever you will it to do.

Light of a Child

When we were children, we were told that the world was our oyster, that we could do anything. We could be energetic, playful, and silly, because we did not limit ourselves. Feeling the grandeur of everything, and wanting to expand out into it, we could experience the wonder of a butterfly and its life of spontaneity. But as adults we get used to the repetitiousness of everyday life, grow bored, and stagnate. If only we knew what type of life was available to us, we would not let our minds get stuck in such ruts.

A Master of the Tao is open to the expansive energy of creation, which makes both the body and mind soft and warm, like that of a child (fig. 1.4). If you are capable of bringing this energy into your heart and brain you will be filled with new life. Then when you see a butterfly you might be as happy and excited as a child. The Tao can open you up to receive the energy of the infinite mind, which can be used wherever it is needed, such as to actualize a vision you have had but could not complete due to lack of ideas and enthusiasm.

When you immerse yourself in the Tao, an abundance of good energy will come your way. As the sacred energy works into your entire being, it will free your mind from all stresses so that you can see life clearly, and be deeply grateful for the life you are able to enjoy. Even at this point you can still cultivate stronger and purer energy; this is why they say the Tao has infinite possibilities. The chi energy is a key to everything, capable of opening any blockage you have in your mind, body, or spirit. It is just a matter of letting the chi marinate into it. Soon the toxic energy will have relaxed away, and the area will be radiating with beautiful energy.

Fig. 1.4. Chi can make the brain and organs soft as a child's.

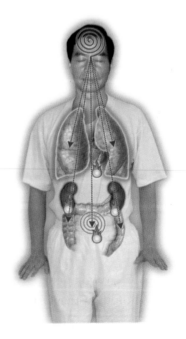

As adults we have the opportunity to be as empty as children, free to experience and explore this vast miracle called life. This potential can reach the far extremities of the planet. Imagine a time when all people will live like this: oceans of people bathing in this most beautiful energy; compassion spilling from everyone's heart. Life can be like a divine dance with everyone and everything. We can know the sun, moon, ocean, forests, and mountains on a personal level, and bathe in everyone's personalized sacred energy, which will keep adding to our own.

The Reason Life Is Simple

You may have felt that living a meaningful life was a distant possibility. But by consciously putting yourself in the Tao, the reason for living will become clear. It just feels so good. When your whole body feels wonderful, soaking in a delicious elixir, you do not have to stress your mind for answers. The reason is simple. Instead of just knowing *of* your spirit, you open your spirit up to be your vessel. Instead of using only your five senses, you explore the senses of your infinite mind. It is a matter of letting all the stresses of life and negative energy seep out of every little corner of your body, until it is as clear as a crystal. The more you remove, the more incredible aspects of human life will appear.

Harmony and Leadership

Energy cultivation will enable you to be much more harmoniously expressive. When the energy has marinated deep enough into your core, you will naturally flow into the position of a talented and beautiful leader. This will not necessarily happen because that was your motive, but because the natural flow in which you have immersed yourself will provide a basis that enables you to come to wise decisions very simply. This is highly valued in today's hectic and confusing world, because just and compassionate decisions bring radiance to all environments.

When energy cultivation makes it possible for the Tao to speak through you, it will naturally make you a more attractive person: pure, simple, and radiant. The Tao will become your actions and your environment. The people that are in your life will come to you through the Tao. As the energy marinates deeper and deeper, it will make your body, meditations, and environment more radiant and pure. This energy will lift you up to feel like a star, which will coat all the places you visit with a pure and enlightened energy.

VIRTUE OF WORLD CONSCIOUSNESS

A major way to refine your chi is to develop your virtue energy. Developing your virtue energy involves being unified with Earth and all its people. When your consciousness expands to encompass the world, your spiritual energy will expand as well. It will naturally change you into a person who can relate with everyone in the world.

Just as you clean your personal body by clearing its blockages, you can extend the same process to the world body, using the meditations in this book. Every continent needs your energy. You can apply chi to the world's blockages, spreading your energy over many people and environments (fig. 1.5). As it expands to encompass millions and millions of people, your beautiful enlightened energy will naturally become vast. When it circulates back toward you, it will be magnified countless times. That will in turn balance your emotions and your whole being. The energy that pulses through you will provide much-needed chi for other parts of our earth body. This will also allow you to communicate with other people with whom you share this beautiful body, as they are also sending chi to it, consciously or unconsciously. When your energy meets theirs, it will generate subtle energy communication.

It is important to know what has caused the blockage of spiritual energy on Earth in order to know how to open the blocks with sincere meditation. It is vital to uncover the truth of how individuals and groups of people have been oppressed, whether by miseducation,

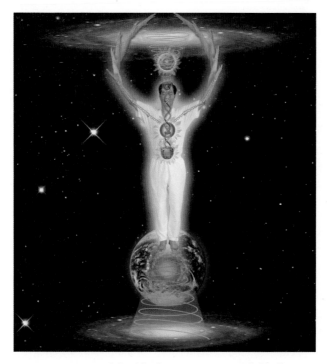

Fig. 1.5. Heal the blockages on our earth body.

war, disease, displacement, or very possibly all of these. Even if you see a trend throughout the world, knowing specific earth "families" will give you a still stronger connection. For example, if you were to think that the poverty of Native American Indians is due to laziness and ignorance, your meditation would not be in harmony with the truth and therefore would not be magnified but blocked. If, however, you were to understand that the impoverishment of Native Americans today is a result of the genocide of 95 percent of their population and the foreign occupation of nearly all their valuable land and resources, then your meditation would be in harmony with the truth and would therefore be strengthened many times.

Knowing the root of the problem will enable you to create a much clearer channel through which you can send healing chi directly from your heart, and a thick steam of compassion from every cell of your being. At the same time, it is a process of cultivating devotion, through

Fig. 1.6. The beautiful spirit of the Buddhist shines
through the page.

which you connect with the enlightened spirits from around the world
in their love, sacred art, and music (fig. 1.6).

Meditating with humility on a specific earth family will help you
to feel the beautiful energy of the calm, enlightened spirits that belong
to that family. You may get radiant visions when you look through
their eyes and see a time when peace and compassion ruled over the
land for hundreds or thousands of years without break. Feel the family around you; do not try to focus too hard but feel the subtle golden
vibration of the people. Let them touch you, whisper to you, and stare
into their deep eyes (fig. 1.7). Use this energy to heal the present day
situation where the energy may be blocked.

There is another very important reason why expanding your
consciousness to embrace the whole world will magnify your spiritual energy. The universe feels safe bestowing such strong energy on
someone if it will benefit the whole earth and not just one person. The

Fig. 1.7. You can get visions of enlightened spirits
when you send healing love energy.

universe does not benefit much if you are cultivating energy simply for
your personal power or pleasure, but the universe will gain a great deal
if you are genuinely working to heal our earth body.

In order to live with world consciousness every day you have
to detach yourself from worldly desires and a focus on the desires
of the spirit. When your actions back up your meditations, you are
being moved by positive energy; you are living the Tao. When you
live the meditations, energy soaks deeper and deeper into your body.
Aligning your actions with the world consciousness might mean
something as simple as being a vessel that represents and speaks
truth, perhaps through spiritual education, environmental work, or
helping to rebuild communities. This requires trust and courage; do
not force the energy but flow with it. Know that you are being aided
and protected by a huge spiritual energy that is alive and has infinite
love for you.

Saturate Your Environment in Chi

The ability to maintain a strong connection with the chi requires trusting the energy. Negative thoughts block the chi from flowing. This is why it is important to make connection to chi a part of your everyday life. You will be in an even better position if you can make it your foundation in life. In fact, it already *is* your foundation; but you need to recognize that this energy is the basis of creation. In order to establish a lasting relationship with chi, it is important to saturate your life in it. This can be done by listening to music that has positive energy, organizing your living space with positive chi, and cultivating relationships with people who have positive chi.

We are coming to a point in the world where it is very important that people who know the truth spread it in their surroundings. This doesn't mean becoming a nuisance by proselytizing, but rather focusing on the nature of energy rather than on materialistic things. If you are in a situation where the only subjects of discussion are materialistic, don't be afraid to remain quiet and focus on what you really want from life. It is much better to say nothing than say things that are not from your heart. Otherwise you can easily be led down a road that is not connected to your heart, instead of fulfilling your desire to represent your true nature.

Focus of the Spirit

Although you may find it awkward to be alone or to remain silent, it is important to keep your focus on what you really desire: a more harmonious life and a more harmonious Earth. It may take a little getting used to, but focusing and working on this vision is very fulfilling. It inspires the mind, relaxes the brain, and puts joy into your heart. Focusing on the true nature of your spirit will cut away past stresses and misconceptions about life, clearing more room for your divine nature to shine through.

When the sacred energy starts pouring out of your entire being

Fig. 1.8. Let the chi expand into your environment.

into the surrounding environment, the energy will only get stronger and continue to pull you deeper into beautiful and divine energy (fig. 1.8). The inner result will be a constant state of strong energy cultivation, eventually resulting in an even higher state of deep relaxation. At this point your energy will be strong enough to achieve any vision you desire, as long as it is aligned with the desires of your spirit. That alignment will naturally allow the energy to keep growing, circulating, and refining, in a continuous cycle that will bring out your highest potential. May you achieve your deepest dream.

Preparing for Meditation

PREPARE A SERENE ENVIRONMENT

It is important to have a comfortable and serene environment when you meditate. The condition of the space will have an impact upon your meditation, because everything carries energy with it (fig. 2.1). If

Fig. 2.1. Creating a serene environment will also create a serene mind.

you are in a cluttered room, you may have a cluttered and busy mind, which blocks deep meditation. Clean the room thoroughly and neatly organize all loose items. If the scent in your room is not attractive, it may also detract from the purity of your meditation. For this you may want to get incense or essential oils. However, if you're in an environment that you cannot change, of course this should not stop you from meditating.

PREPARE YOURSELF

Along with preparing your environment, you also need to prepare your body for meditation.

Eat Consciously

Be conscious of the food that you eat. Eat plenty of vegetables, which add a lot of oxygen, vitamins, and minerals to your body. If you eat too much meat it will clog your intestines and hamper your lower abdomen breathing. Meats contain significant amounts of growth hormones and chemicals, so fish is usually a better alternative. Chewing your food well allows your body to absorb more of the nutrients it contains and helps it to flow through the intestines with more ease. Avoid eating one hour to one and a half hours before meditation. This will allow time for the food to be digested and provide for comfortable lower abdomen breathing.

Take a Shower

It is also important to shower before you meditate. Just like cleansing your environment, showering before meditation helps to put your mind in a clean state of being. Even if you are used to showering after practice in the morning, you will see that showering before helps to keep in the serene energy you have acquired in meditation.

Wear Comfortable Clothing

Meditate in the right clothing. When you meditate you should wear loose clothing, which allows the energy to flow freely throughout your body. That will foster good blood circulation to open the channels. You should also wear clothing of natural fibers. When you meditate your pores open up and the skin is sensitive to the materials it contacts; natural fibers are more comfortable to the skin.

Warm Up the Body for Good Meditation

Warming up is an essential part of the meditation process. It creates balanced energy in all your muscles and strengthens the circulation of blood and energy. The Universal Tao recommends doing some stretching, Tai Chi, and Chi Kung, which are effective ways to get your body, mind, and spirit ready for meditation. These practices will make you more sensitive to chi, therefore deepening your meditations. The most important part of the body to loosen is the spine. If your spine is tense, it will greatly inhibit the circulation of energy to the rest of your body. Also make sure your lower abdomen is relaxed so that your Bellows Breathing is not blocked.

THE CORRECT POSTURE FOR MEDITATION

Aligning your posture is the first step in starting to meditate. A correct posture is one in which your skeleton is aligned in a way that promotes energy circulation and unifies your body into one flowing unit. The most importing thing to know about posture is that it needs to be relaxed. If your body is not relaxed your mind will not be able to relax and feel the energy. You also want your body to be firmly planted and stable. A stable posture allows you to meditate for longer periods of time (fig. 2.2).

A correct posture is achieved by paying attention to several key aspects of the body, including your feet, sitz bones, spine, shoulders, and head.

Base: The foundation of the meditation posture is your base, which consists of your feet and your sitz bones, the points most receptive to earth energy. On the soles of your feet are the Bubbling Spring points (Yung Chuan), two of the four points most sensitive to chi, along with points on your hands. They are like sensitive antennae. The Bubbling Spring points are very good at sucking up Earth's energy and dispelling large amounts of toxic energy.

For the Fusion meditation we recommend you sit on a straight-backed chair. Place your feet shoulder-width apart, with your feet straight, forming the number 11. Make sure your Bubbling Spring points are touching the floor. Your feet should be directly under your knees so your calves are straight. If the floor is not carpeted and is cold, place a towel beneath your feet.

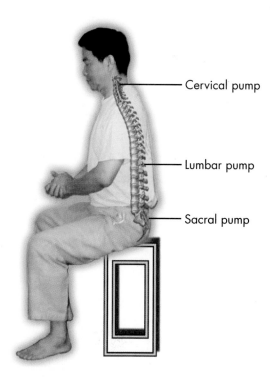

Fig. 2.2. Correct posture creates optimum
potential of energy flow.

Sit directly on your sitz bones, and avoid leaning back on your tailbone (coccyx). Leaning on your tailbone will put pressure on your sacrum, a major pump for the cerebrospinal fluid, which is essential for experiencing deep absorption. Put your weight on top of your sitz bones and make sure it is spread equally between them and the Bubbling Spring points.

Hands: Relax your hands and let them rest in your lap, clasped lightly together with the right palm over the left palm and the right thumb and forefinger wrapped around the base of the left thumb. The clasped hand position works especially well to generate and balance energy during meditation.

Spine: Your spine should be straight and relaxed. If your spine gets tired during longer rounds of meditation it means that you need to transfer the weight from the muscles in your back to your spinal column, which is designed to hold hundreds of pounds. This is done by imagining a string attached to the top of your head pulling upward, elongating your spine. This will increase the space between each of the vertebrae so they are not putting pressure on each other. Make an extra effort to stretch the top of the spine where it meets the head at the C7 point (Jade Pillow). To do this, pull your chin back slightly. This will create a strong energy line along the whole spine.

Your spinal column houses many nerves, and it is also the main pathway in the Microcosmic Orbit. If your spine is relaxed, energy will flow up it freely. Practicing Iron Shirt Chi Kung is an invaluable technique to build great alignment and posture.

Shoulders: Your shoulders should be slightly pulled back so they do not pull on your spine. There should be about an inch of space in your armpits for free circulation. Whenever we feel stress in life, the first place it goes is to our shoulders, so it is very important in meditation for our shoulders to feel very relaxed.

Chin: To open the C7 point, pull your chin back slightly, just enough so that your ears are over your shoulders. This will also prevent your head from leaning forward and pulling the spine out of alignment.

Eyes: Your eyes should generally be closed or slightly open. If you feel sleepy or distracted, you may want to open your eyes for a while until you regain focus.

Tongue: The tip of your tongue should be lightly touching the upper palate. This connection functions like an energy switch connecting the Tu Mo and Ren Mo, the Governor and Functional Channels.

Special Power of the Pakua

The pakua is a power symbol that encompasses the eight forces of nature (fig. 3.1). *Pa* means "eight" and *kua* is "symbol." The eight forces that the pakua holds are *kan* (water), *li* (fire), *chen* (thunder), *tui* (lake, rain), *kun* (earth), *ken* (mountain), *sun* (wind), and *chien* (wood). Each force corresponds to a particular organ and to one of the five senses as well. The eight forces, like the five elements, are the result of the interplay of yin and yang.

The pakua is a symbol you can easily manipulate in your mind to extract the pure energies of nature. By activating and cultivating the ancient pakua, you will be able to harness nature's power to detoxify and purify the energies of your body, mind, and spirit. Another amaz-

Fig. 3.1. The pakua gives you powerful access to the eight forces.

ing benefit is being able to communicate with each of these forces; when you get to know them you will feel a divine connection between the eight forces and your organs and senses.

CHANTING

Chanting the names of the eight forces will enable you to establish a strong connection with their energy more quickly. Chanting aids in getting to know the energy on a deeper level because the Chinese name has a rhythmic connection to the element that helps to unlock its power. By calling the name of a force, you are calling the energy to be activated and move in the organ, the sense, and the element with which it is related. Another important aspect is that chanting gives the mind physical control instead of relying only on the chi energy, which is not something you can manipulate as readily as the power of the word.

Chanting the names of the forces also empowers vibration, especially when you make sure that the sound is coming from your lower tan tien. You will know that you have established a good connection when you feel your voice connected to your sexual energy, which is the essence of the lower tan tien. You will feel the word vibrating through your lower abdomen, sexual organs, and—when it is really activated—through your whole body (fig. 3.2). At this point chanting will bring you into a sweet

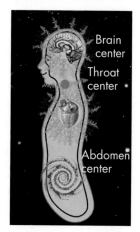

Brain center

Throat center •

Abdomen center

Fig. 3.2. The word vibrates your whole being, especially the designated point.

tranquil state, where the only thing on your mind is the divine energy, which will cause your body to keep buzzing in the vibration.

SYMBOLISM

For this practice you have to be able keep your mind on one mental image—in this case the pakua—for extended periods of time. When you have visualized it enough times it will just float into your mind by habit. Keeping your mind focused on an image is as easy as focusing on the energy that is connected to the symbol. The best way to focus on the energy of an entire pakua is to focus on the elemental force of each trigram independently, then connect them.

When you visualize the elemental force of a given trigram, you are connecting a particular energy to it. For example, the trigram chen is thunder and lightning. When you connect your liver and eyes to this energy and marinate them in it, that will promote strong cleansing and refining of the liver and eye energy. Afterward, every time you visualize the chen trigram, it will emit this same strong vibration to you. This is the power of symbolism: "a picture is worth a thousand words." It is beautiful in that it is so stimulating. After you establish this connection with each of the eight trigrams, just looking at the pakua will automatically elicit a powerful energy comprised of a blend of these eight forces. Just looking at the pakua will draw negative energies out and fill your organs and senses with a pure and refreshing vitality.

A great way to imprint the pakua on your memory is by drawing it directly on your abdomen, or on a piece of paper that you hold or tape to your abdomen. The yin of the Tai Chi symbol is of course blue for water and the yang is red for fire. The trigrams are composed of three lines, each of which is designated either as yin, a broken (blue) line, or yang, a solid (red) line. The frame can be drawn black.

The location of the pakua should not be visualized on the skin but 1½ inches (3.8 centimeters) under the surface. The front pakua is between the underside of the rib cage and just above the pubic bone. The rear pakua is in the same position on the back.

ACTIVATING THE PAKUA PRACTICE

In the pakua practice we begin with chanting the name of the particular trigram we are focusing on to activate it. Then we chant the designation of the three lines that compose it. Particular hand movements are coordinated with the chanting of yin and yang for the lines. While chanting *yin*, you want to connect your antennae-like hands to the cosmic or heavenly energy (fig. 3.3). Chant *yin* until you feel you have gathered sufficient energy, then contract the energy down into your lower tan tien. While chanting *yang*, start at the lower tan tien and expand out into the cosmos, as the essence of yang is to expand (fig. 3.4).

Fig. 3.3. Chant *yin* as you collect energy from the cosmos, then compact it into your lower tan tien.

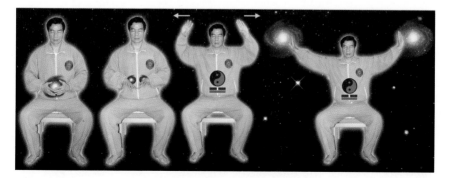

Fig. 3.4. While chanting *yang*, gather energy in the lower tan tien and expand it out into the cosmos.

Trigrams of the Pakua

 Kan: The First Sound

Kan (yin yang yin) is the power symbol of the element water, the gathering yin power, connected to the kidneys, ears, and sexual organs (fig. 3.5). To evoke the energy of the symbol, look down, touch the lower section of your abdomen with your right hand, and chant *kan* several times until you feel energy moving in your kidneys, ears, and sexual organs. Then chant the lines of the trigram, beginning with the inner line, the one closest to the Tai Chi symbol: *yin, yang, yin.*

Fig. 3.5. The kan trigram is a symbol for water gathering power.

 Li: The Second Sound

Li (yang yin yang) is the symbol of fire (fig. 3.6). It represents the tongue connecting to the heart, the prospering power. Look up, touching the right hand to the upper abdominal region and chant *li* until you feel the fire moving upward through your chest. Then chant *yang, yin, yang* for the lines of the trigram.

Fig. 3.6. The li
trigram is a symbol
for fire.

☯ Chen: The Third Sound

Yin
Yin
Yang

Chen (yang yin yin) is the symbol of thunder and lightning (fig. 3.7).
It represents the liver and eyes, the wood element, and the generating
power. With your eyes looking to the right and your hand touching the
right abdomen, chant *chen* (pronounced "djen") until it activates your
liver and eyes. Then chant the lines of the trigram, beginning with the
inner line, the one closest to the Tai Chi symbol: *yang, yin, yin.*

Lightning and thunder in
the forest

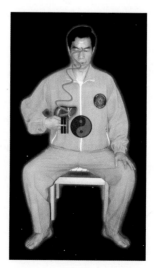

Fig. 3.7. The chen trigram is a symbol
for thunder and lightning.

☯ Tui: The Fourth Sound

		Yin
		Yang
		Yang

Tui (yang yang yin) represents the lake and rain (fig. 3.8). It connects to the lungs and nose, the yin side of the metal element, and contracting power. With your eyes looking to the left, and your hand touching the left side of your abdomen, chant *tui* (pronounced "tway") until the energy is activated. Then chant the lines of the trigram, beginning with the inner line: *yang, yang, yin.*

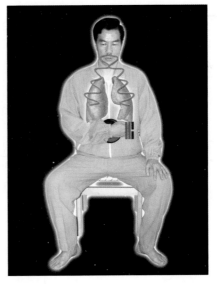

Fig. 3.8. The tui trigram is a symbol for the lake and rain.

☯ Kun: The Fifth Sound

		Yin
		Yin
		Yin

Kun (yin yin yin) is the symbol of the earth (fig. 3.9). It connects to the stomach, spleen, and pancreas. While looking to the left and touching the upper left abdomen, chant *kun* until you feel the energies in the organs activated. Then chant *yin, yin, yin.*

Fig. 3.9. The kun trigram is a symbol for the earth.

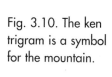 *Ken: The Sixth Sound*    Yang
Yin
Yin

Ken (yin yin yang) is the symbol representing the mountain and the yin side of water power (fig. 3.10). It is connected to the bladder and sexual organs. Chant *ken* until activation. Then chant *yin, yin, yang*.

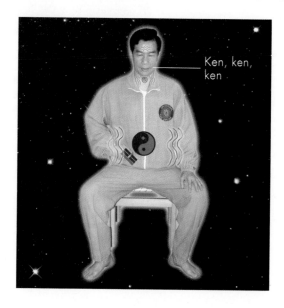

Fig. 3.10. The ken trigram is a symbol for the mountain.

❂ *Sun: The Seventh Sound*

▬▬▬▬▬	Yang
▬▬▬▬▬	Yang
▬▬ ▬▬	Yin

Sun (yin yang yang) represents wind (fig. 3.11). It is connected to the gallbladder and wood power. While looking to the right and touching the upper right of your abdomen, picture the symbol on the upper right corner of the abdominal pakua. Chant *sun*, then chant *yin, yang, yang.*

Sun, sun, sun

Fig. 3.11. The sun trigram is a symbol for the wind.

❂ *Chien: The Eighth Sound*

▬▬▬▬▬	Yang
▬▬▬▬▬	Yang
▬▬▬▬▬	Yang

Chien (yang yang yang) represents heaven and the yang side of the metal element (fig. 3.12). It is connected with the large intestine. While looking to the left and touching the lower left section of the abdominal pakua, chant *chien* until you feel the energy connect to the large intestine. Then chant *yang, yang, yang.*

Fig. 3.12. The chien trigram is a symbol for heaven.

Chien, chien, chien

🌀 Connect all Eight Trigrams Together

This is a very important step because it connects the eight trigrams of the pakua into a unified symbol (fig. 3.13). Each trigram in the pakua should feel solid, indicating that it has a mature relationship with

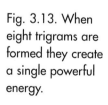

Fig. 3.13. When eight trigrams are formed they create a single powerful energy.

Tai Chi, Tai Chi, Tai Chi

the pakua. As the pakua spins you should feel a divine blending of all the forces. This feeling can be intensely beautiful if the connections between all the trigrams are well saturated.

Chant *Tai Chi* until you feel the symbol spinning in the middle of your pakua. The front Tai Chi spins counterclockwise if female and clockwise if male. Slowly chant *kan* (water), *li* (fire), *chen* (thunder and lightning), *tui* (lake, rain), *kun* (earth), *ken* (mountain), *sun* (wind), and *chien* (heaven) until you feel the divine energies blending. Then allow the pakua to spiral a little faster until you have a good grip on the divine pearl of refined, balanced energy that is created. Then chant the trigram names several more times.

Forming Four Pakuas and Establishing the Cauldron

◉ Form a Pakua on the Back

Forming the back pakua is simple because you just copy the front pakua onto your back, directly behind your navel. The back Tai Chi symbol spins in the opposite direction from the one in the front. Slowly connect your chanting to the visualization of the eight forces. Slowly chant *kan, li, chen, tui, kun, ken, sun,* and *chien* until you feel all eight forces blending on your back.

◉ Form a Right and Left Pakua

The right pakua is a copy of the back pakua moved to the right side, and the left pakua is a copy of the front, both at the same level as the front and back pakuas.

◉ Collecting Pakuas in the Cauldron

Focus on each of the four pakuas. When you focus on them, they will start spiraling on their own and suck all the toxins out of your

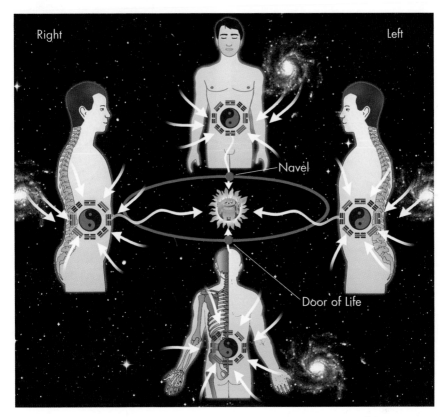

Fig. 3.14. All pakuas going into the cauldron generate a powerful energy.

five senses and your organs. Each will create a pearl of radiant and stimulating energy. Feel the lower tan tien suck these four pearls and all of the energy into its center to create one dynamic pearl. Take this pearl through the Microcosmic Orbit and feel its powerful energy (fig. 3.14).

Forming the Heart Center Pakua

In order to form the heart center pakua, visualize it as you focus on your heart. The heart center pakua is the reverse of the abdominal pakua. You will feel the space around your heart getting bigger and the ancient pakua will start to spiral. As it spirals it will create an electromagnetic

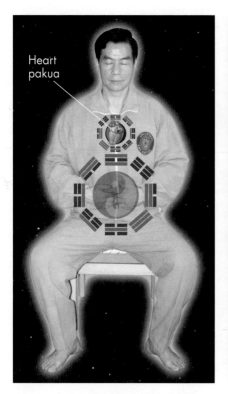
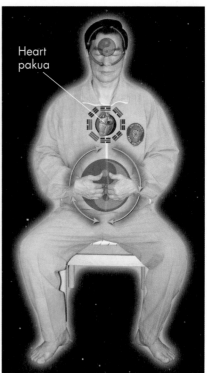

Fig. 3.15. The pakuas create another divine energy.

field that you will feel radiating around your chest and body (fig. 3.15). Chant the names of the eight forces: *kan, li, chen, tui, kun, ken, sun,* and *chien* until you feel all the trigrams activated. Then relax and feel the energy spiraling in your heart tan tien. When you feel you have created a divine and powerful energy, let it drain into your lower tan tien. Stay connected with the powerful energy.

Forming the Four Pakuas of the Head
Forming the Facial Pakua

The pakua on your face is also the reverse of the abdominal pakua, so chen is on the left and tui is on the right. The other trigrams are

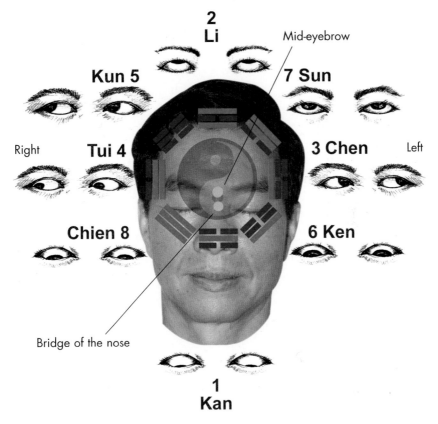

Fig. 3.16. The facial pakuas can really activate
your five senses.

arranged accordingly (fig. 3.16). The Tai Chi symbol centers on your
mid-eyebrow and spans up to the forehead and down to the bridge of
the nose. Do the chanting in the same way as with the front pakua,
while touching the part of the face where the trigram you are chanting is located. When you rest after making each specific sound, feel
that the symbol of the trigram is imprinted on the forehead. Let
each trigram expand far out into the universe, then come back to
your body. When it returns it will have picked up a huge amount of
energy.

❀ Creating the Pakuas on the Back of the Head and the Left and Right Sides

The front facial pakua is transferred to the back of the head, where it spins in the opposite direction. Just as with the abdominal pakuas, the rear pakua is copied to form the pakua on the right side of the head, and the front pakua is copied to the left side. When they are all activated, the crystal room of the mid-brain will spiral faster and faster, purifying and filtering the energy in your head.

Building the
Compassion Fire

Compassion is reality. Compassion is loving all humans, moon, sun, forests, and yourself with the same essential energy, an energy that originates in the heart and flows through every opening of your body. Compassion is not a subtle love for all, but rather a strong love that takes your full attention. It is an intense feeling in which all negative thoughts are dissolved in the strong vibration of love (fig. 4.1).

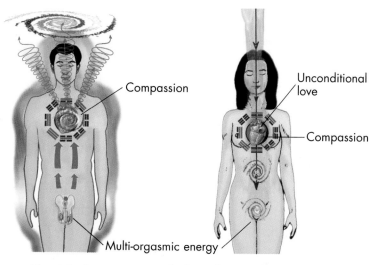

Fig. 4.1. Compassion is a feeling of intense love.

Compassion is a feeling of being at one with everything. Your body and mind become so sensitive to energy that you are able to feel that all of our spirits are made of the same beautiful energy. It is not a question of "thinking" of our divine connection; it is a matter of feeling it as strongly as you feel water when you are floating in it. When you are full of compassion you cannot entertain negative, divisive thoughts. It would be like purposefully stopping the best massage of your life after a short minute.

Compassion is the way to be in love with each moment of life, as we were meant to be.

When compassion arises in you it may feel like a fountain spraying out of the depths of your heart; when it reaches your third eye your whole body will be immersed. At this point you will feel like a baby in heaven, where the oxygen you breathe and the landscape around you are a delicious elixir. The wind might feel like it goes through you like a feather. Compassion will make your whole body extremely relaxed and warm and give you the sensation that your whole body is melting into everything (fig. 4.2).

It is possible that some people around you will not understand why you feel the way you do, but do not let this distract you, because it can take away from your state of relaxation. Give these people a hug or reason with them, so as to immerse them in the flow of love. At this point it is very possible that you will intuitively sense the sad or sick energies within others, because you will feel their blockages as yours as you "melt" into them. Of course you will not receive their blockages, as long as you clear the energy (fig. 4.3). This heightened sensitivity is the reason why people who become genuinely compassionate tend to get into fields of body, mind, and spirit education, helping the poor and sick: they have an abundance of love to give. They can do more than a person in these fields who lacks compassion because the energy they have activated gives them true insight into the potential of their true self.

Fig. 4.2. Being at one feels as though you are melting into everything.

Fig. 4.3. Do not let people's negative vibrations affect your divine feeling.

HOW TO CULTIVATE COMPASSION

The cultivation of compassion involves activating the energy of the organs in the Creation Cycle (the sexual organs, heart, spleen, lungs, kidneys, and liver). If you smile or laugh into the organs, it opens their pores and relaxes and massages them. This fosters the release of any blockages, inflexibilities, or stagnant emotions that interfere with the expression of positive emotions and virtues by the organs and the channels that connect them.

First you put orgasmic energy in all the organs to massage them. Then you blend the energy of the organs in your lower tan tien (fig. 4.4). When you raise that energy through your Microcosmic Orbit to the pineal gland it will open the dam of your compassion energy.

When you mix your purified emotions with your orgasmic chi your whole body will be charged with an ecstatic energy, which feels so good that you will naturally experience a strong love for life and all the seeds that have grown from it.

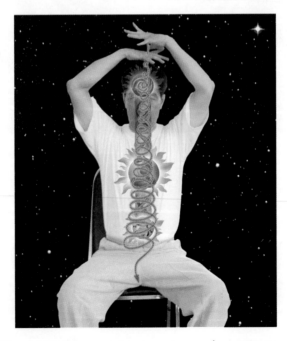

Fig. 4.4. Build orgasmic energy in your lower tan tien.

FORMULA FOR LASTING COMPASSION

Compassion is made lasting by charging it with orgasmic energy. At a certain level in your practice, orgasmic energy will flow through your body every time you meditate, and remain with you throughout the day (fig. 4.5). The fusion of orgasmic energy and compassion energy allows you to circulate them both while you meditate. This refines and cultivates the energy at higher levels so your body's vibration grows stronger and stronger.

Like love, compassion energy has no limits regarding how strong it can get. As you carry it longer and longer it will keep getting more refined and will carry more intelligence and experience. As you keep charging your organs, which will become second nature, the compassion energy will both marinate deeper and deeper into your core and grow more expansive. Like orgasmic energy, it has infinite potential:

Fig. 4.5. You can carry compassion with you all day and night.

Fig. 4.6. There is no limit to the strength of love for
our Earth.

there is no limit to how powerfully and well we can love Earth and its
beings (fig. 4.6).

This compassion energy is the major energy for all the Fusion
techniques and higher practices of Kan and Li. Compassion is the
most important energy of transformation and will be used in all the
practices.

PRACTICE

First start with lower abdomen breathing. Bring the breath down to
the lower abdomen until it reaches the sexual organs. If you are doing
the breathing properly your breath should circulate into your sexual
organs. You should feel warm blood and something like electricity

rush through them. You should also feel them stretch as you inhale, and contract as you exhale. This will easily energize the organs in your lower abdomen. At this point your anus muscle should be tight, so that it will create a bridge for the powerful energy to flow into your sacrum and then into your spine. Continue doing the belly breathing until you feel strong sexual energy circulating with each new breath. This sexual energy is the energetic make up of your lower tan tien.

 ## Creating Compassion and Orgasm in the Organs

1. Smile the multi-orgasmic energy into the heart until you feel it soften with deep love (fig. 4.7).

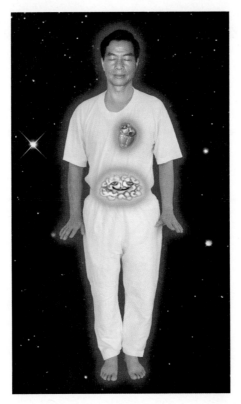

Fig. 4.7. Free your mind and let your heart
relax deeply.

2. Connect the lower tan tien to the universe and feel the compassion energy flow in (fig. 4.8).

Fig. 4.8. Feel the energies from the depths of the universe enter.

3. Smile the multi-orgasmic energy into the spleen and let the joyous love of the heart activate openness and fairness (fig. 4.9). Let the yellow light flow in from above.

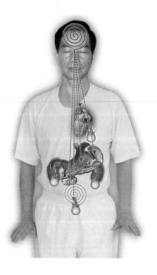

Fig. 4.9. Free your mind and let the spleen relax deeply.

4. Smile or laugh the multi-orgasmic energy into the lungs and large intestine (fig. 4.10). Send the divine love from within your heart to the lungs to activate courage and righteousness. Let the white light flow in from above.

Fig. 4.10. Free your mind and create intense healing energy in your lungs and large intestine.

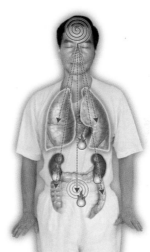

5. Let the divine love of your heart activate the gentleness, softness, and calmness within the kidneys (fig. 4.11). Let the blue light flow in from the universe.

Fig. 4.11. Relax your mind and let the energy spiral deep into your kidneys.

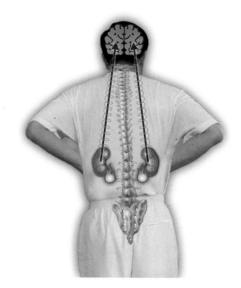

6. Smile and laugh the multi-orgasmic energy into your liver and gallbladder, so they are relaxed and vibrant (fig. 4.12). Let the love in the heart activate the kindness and generosity of your liver. Let the green light flow in from the depths of the universe.

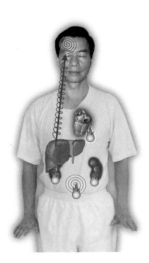

Fig. 4.12. Relax your mind and spiral the energy into the depths of your liver.

7. Smile and laugh the multi-orgasmic energy into your heart and feel all the virtuous energy from all the organs go into the heart, spiraling and blending into one compassionate energy (fig. 4.13). Feel the multicolored light spectrum come down from the heavens.

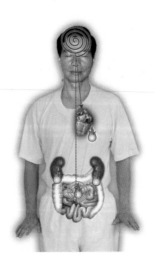

Fig. 4.13. Let the radiant energies from the organs penetrate deeply as they spiral into your accepting heart.

8. Smile and laugh the multi-orgasmic energy into your whole being and let the compassion energy radiate throughout (fig. 4.14).

Fig. 4.14. Let the multi-orgasmic energy radiate out from the core of your being.

9. Smile and laugh the multi-orgasmic energy into the universe, then let the energy from within radiate out into the depths of the universe (fig. 4.15).

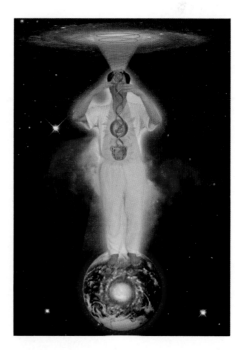

Fig. 4.15. Send the multi-orgasmic energy out into the depths of the universe.

10. Let the healing multi-orgasmic energies of the deep, deep universe pour back into your body until it overflows (fig. 4.16).

Fig. 4.16. Free your mind; the universe is too big for a closed mind to feel, so let the energy grow as big as you are free to imagine.

11. Smile and laugh the multi-orgasmic energy into your sexual organs; send the divine energy into all your sexual organs and grow the energy (fig. 4.17).

Fig. 4.17. Send the healing energies into the sexual organs.

Introduction to Fusion of the Eight Psychic Channels

Fusion of the Eight Psychic Channels is the last part of the Fusion practices. It teaches the final techniques and meditations needed to prepare you for the higher practices of the Immortal Tao. Fusion of the Eight Psychic Channels includes the following practices:

1. Opening and cleaning the Great Bridge and the Great Regulator Channel. Both consist of a yin and a yang channel. Together they form four channels (Yin and Yang Wei and the Yin and Yang Chiao Channels). They are the last extraordinary (psychic) acupuncture channels to open. The others are: the Governor (Du Mai) Channel and Functional (Ren Mai) Channel of the Microcosmic Orbit; the Thrusting Channels (which count as one channel, related to the Chong Mai); and the Belt Channel (related to the Dai Mai).

2. Learning to protect your spine and energy field, clear your senses, drill your head with energy, and seal your aura.

3. Learning to form an energy body and transfer the Microcosmic Orbit, the Thrusting Channels, and the Belt Channel to it.

THE GREAT BRIDGE CHANNEL AND
THE GREAT REGULATOR CHANNEL

The routes followed by the Great Regulator and Great Bridge Channels lie close together. They have no points of their own, but run across specific points of the twelve organ meridians. In this way they connect all the organ meridians, enabling the energy to flow from one meridian to another, and for it to be balanced and regulated. The Great Bridge Channel (Yin and Yang Chiao Mai) serves to connect all the meridians. The Great Regulator Channel (Yin and Yang Wei Mai) serves to regulate, coordinate, and balance the energy flow between the meridians, also called the body's channels.

Although they are separate channels, in Fusion of the Eight Psychic Channels the Great Regulator and Great Bridge Channels are treated as one channel with a yin and a yang part. The yin part connects all the yin organ meridians and regulates the flow of energy in them, the yang part connects all the yang organ meridians and regulates the flow of energy in them. The yin channels run along the inside of the legs and arms and the front of the body. They also regulate the blood. The yang channels run on the outside of the legs and arms and the back of the body. They control defensive energy and regulate resistance to external infections. In other words, the yin channels protect the body from "attacks" from within and the yang channels protect the body from external "attacks."

The most important reasons to open the Bridge and Regulator Channels are to promote the unimpeded flow of energy in the body, to heal the body, and to prepare it to receive and to circulate the higher energy forces of the Immortal Tao practices. All eight psychic channels act as receivers and distributors of the universal force to the organs and glands. For this reason, working with the eight psychic channels is considered spiritual work in the Taoist system.

Forming the control base of the eight psychic channels is the Gate of Life and Death (also known as the Gate of Mortality) at the Perineum point. The Perineum point serves many purposes. It is considered the sexual energy base. It is also the point that is connected to the Bubbling Spring points, the collection points for the earth energy that are on the soles of the feet. The Belt Channel passes through the Perineum point as it connects the other seven channels. The interconnection of the Belt Channel makes it possible to move the energy from one channel to any other channel, while it serves to protect all the body's centers. The Crown point at the pineal gland is the other common point of the eight psychic channels.

LOCATING THE POINTS OF THE GREAT BRIDGE AND GREAT REGULATOR CHANNELS

The following section identifies all the points of these channels, along with their locations and their meaning as acupuncture points.* After locating and becoming familiar with the points, you will be ready to proceed with the procedures given in chapter six.

Yang Points on the Head: GB 17 to ST 4

GB 17 (Gall Bladder Meridian)
Traditional Name: Cheng Yin = Correct Management
Location: Slightly behind the center of the top of the head, and to the right and left sides (see fig. 5.1 on page 50).
Uses: To help relieve headaches and toothaches.

GB 16 (Gall Bladder Meridian)
Traditional Name: Mu Chuang = Eye Window
Location: On top of the head at the central point, and to the right and left sides (see fig. 5.1 on page 50).
Uses: To help relieve eye problems and facial edema (swelling through water retention).

---

*The acupuncture point locations in this book are part of the Universal Tao System. They may differ slightly from point locations found in other texts.

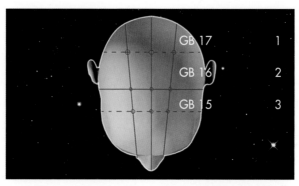

Fig. 5.1. Yang points on the top of the head

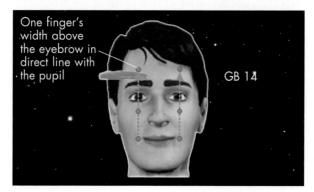

Fig. 5.2. The location of point GB 14 (Gall Bladder meridian)

GB 15 *(Gall Bladder Meridian)*

Traditional Name: Lin Chi = Temporarily Weeping

Location: On top of the head in front of the central point, and to the right and left sides (fig. 5.1).

Uses: To help relieve eye problems, a stuffy nose, and strokes.

GB 14 *(Gall Bladder Meridian)*

Traditional Name: Yang Pai = White Yang or Pure Yang

Location: One finger's width above the eyebrow directly in line with the pupil of the eye (fig. 5.2).

Uses: To help relieve eye problems such as glaucoma and night blindness, forehead pain, facial nerve paralysis, stuffy nose, and strokes.

ST 2 (Stomach Meridian)

Traditional Name: Szu Pai = Four White

Location: Below the eye, straight down from the pupil (fig. 5.3).

Uses: To help relieve eye disease, toothaches, facial nerve paralysis, nose bleeds, and colds.

ST 4 (Stomach Meridian)

Traditional Name: Ti Tsang = Ground Storehouse

Location: At the intersection point of a line straight down from the pupil to the base of the cheekbone, and another line along the curve of the cheekbone (fig. 5.3).

Uses: To help clear nasal passages and relieve colds, toothaches, eye problems, facial paralysis, nose bleeds, and runny nose.

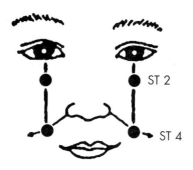

Fig. 5.3. The location of ST 2 and ST 4 (Stomach meridian)

The Entire Front (Yin) Route of the Channel: CV 23 to KD 1

CV 23 (Conception Vessel or Functional Channel)

Traditional Name: Lien Chuan = Corner Spring

Location: Behind the midpoint of the lower edge of the chin bone. Hook the thumb behind the bone and press upward and forward (see fig. 5.5 on page 53).

Uses: To help relieve laryngitis and clear the throat.

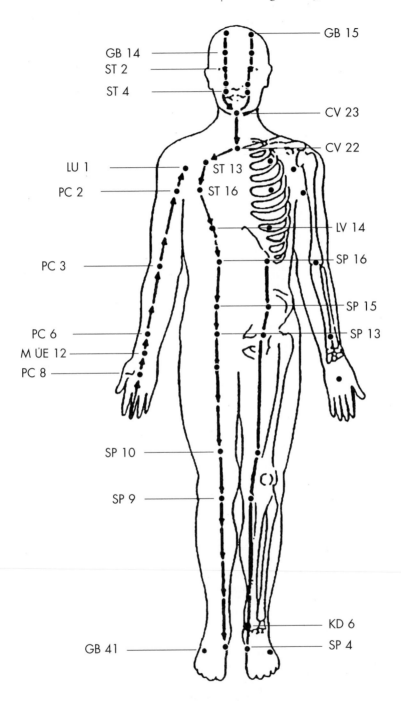

Fig. 5.4. The yin side of the body

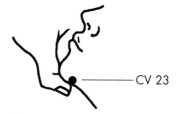

Fig. 5.5. The location of CV 23 (Conception
Vessel or Functional Channel)

CV 22 (Conception Vessel or Functional Channel)

Traditional Name: Tien Tu = Celestial Protrusion

Location: At the top of the breastbone (sternum) in the V-shaped
indentation; press downward at a 45-degree angle (fig. 5.6).

Uses: To relieve asthma, bronchitis, coughing, sore throat, and lar-
ynx spasms. Pressing and releasing CV 22 can cause energy to flow
more easily through the chest, thereby helping to restore proper
breathing.

Fig. 5.6. The location
of CV 22 (Conception
Vessel or Functional
Channel)

ST 13 (Stomach Meridian)

Traditional Name: Chi Hu = Door of Chi

Location: Below the midpoint of the collarbone between the first and
second ribs. Press straight into the body. The point will feel sore
or will produce a sensation like an electric shock (fig. 5.7).

Fig. 5.7. The
location of ST 13
(Stomach meridian)

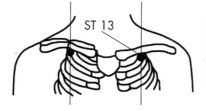

Below the
collarbone
between
the first and
second ribs

Uses: To relieve asthma, bronchitis, chest and back pain, and hiccups. Unrestricted flow through ST 13 allows good energy to flow through the chest.

ST 16 (Stomach Meridian)

Traditional Name: Yin Chuang = Breast Window

Location: Between the third and fourth ribs, one rib directly above the nipples in males, slightly higher in females (fig. 5.8). When pressed, the point feels somewhat sore, especially on females.

Uses: To relieve coughing, asthma, swelling of the breast, chest and stomach pain, heartburn, shortness of breath, and melancholy. Good energy flow clears the whole breast region and promotes optimism.

LV 14 (Liver Meridian)

Traditional Name: Chi Men = Gate of Hope

Location: On the mamillary line, 2 to 3 inches directly below the nipple in the space between the sixth and seventh ribs. Follow the bottom edge of the rib cage from the sternum until the first major indentation, then trace a line down from the nipples. The intersection is the LV 14 area (fig. 5.8). Press slightly up and into the abdomen. The point will feel quite sore when pressed.

Uses: To relieve difficulty in breathing, chest pain, diarrhea, cholera, menopausal disorders, childbirth pains, and abdominal tension. Pressing LV 14 affects the liver, gallbladder, and diaphragm. Used traditionally to relieve side aches from too much running, and to relieve hiccups, belching, and snoring.

SP 16 (Spleen Meridian)

Traditional Name: Fu Ai = Abdominal Sorrow

Location: Below the bottom edge of the rib cage directly in line with the nipple (fig. 5.8). For women, it is in line with ST 13 under the collarbone, and just below LV 14 at the edge of the bottom

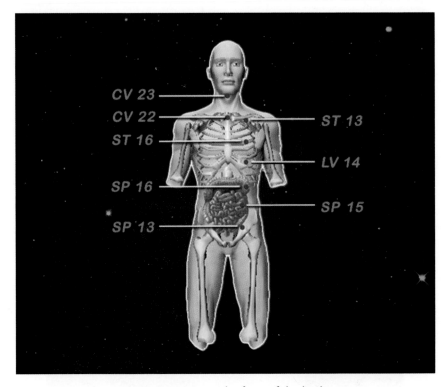

Fig. 5.8. Points on the front of the body

rib. For men, it is in line with ST 13 and ST 16, just beneath the rib cage.

Uses: To relieve abdominal pain, constipation, and dysentery.

SP 15 (Spleen Meridian)

Traditional Name: Da Heng = Big Horizontal

Location: To the sides of the navel directly in line with the nipple (fig. 5.8).

Uses: To relieve nervousness, dysentery, constipation, excessive sweating, diarrhea, abdominal pain, and intestinal paralysis.

SP 13 (Spleen Meridian)

Traditional Name: Fu She = Palace Dwelling

Location: Two fingers' width above the horizontal midline of the pubic area (fig. 5.9). Hold this point firmly without excessive pressure; it may feel ticklish.

Uses: To relieve abdominal pain and tension, colic pain, appendicitis, and constipation. Good energy flow through SP 13 relaxes the abdominal region, groin, thigh, and sexual organs; it relieves menstrual cramps, indigestion, and intestinal weakness.

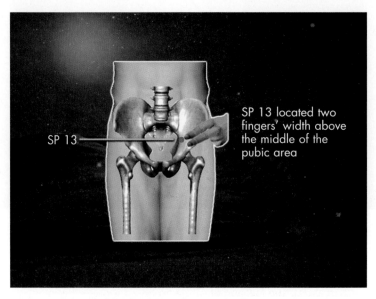

SP 13

SP 13 located two fingers' width above the middle of the pubic area

Fig. 5.9. The location of SP 13 (Spleen meridian)

SP 10 (Spleen Meridian)

Traditional Name: Hseuh Hai = Sea of Blood

Location: Three fingers' width above the knee on the inside of the thigh (fig. 5.10). Place the left palm on the kneecap, fingers pointing to the inside of the knee. Press down on the inside with the thumb. The point is sensitive to pressure.

Uses: To relieve abnormal menstrual flow and cramps, uterine bleeding, rashes, and indigestion. Good energy flow through SP 10 promotes smooth functioning of the female organs. This point also releases the flow of energy through the thighs and knees.

SP 9 (Spleen Meridian)

Traditional Name: Yin Lin Chuan = Dark Tomb Spring

Location: On the inside of the leg below the top of the tibia bone (the large bone of the leg) (fig. 5.10). The point is very tender.

Uses: To relieve abdominal pain and distension, excessive menstrual flow, menstrual pain, lower back pain, and swelling. Unrestricted energy flow through SP 9 increases the flow of energy through the knees and legs.

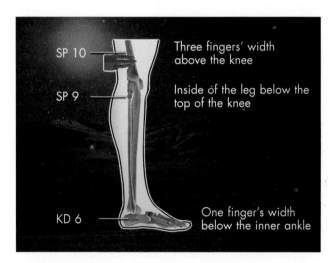

Fig. 5.10. The location of SP 9 and SP 10 (Spleen meridian) and KD 6 (Kidney meridian)

KD 6 (Kidney Meridian)

Traditional Name: Chao Hai = Shining Sea

Location: One finger's width below the inner ankle (fig. 5.10). The point is sensitive to pressure.

Uses: To relieve mental disorders, insomnia, tonsillitis, menstrual disorders, epilepsy, and sadness. This point helps balance the yin aspect of the Great Bridge Channel. When good energy flows through KD 6, problems in the female sexual organs and the kidneys will be reduced. Also, a deep refreshing sleep is encouraged by pressing this point.

SP 4 (Spleen Meridian)

Traditional Name: Kung Sun = Grandson

Location: On the bottom of the foot, in a hollow behind the joint of the big toe (fig. 5.11). The point is sensitive to pressure.

Uses: To relieve heart pain, stomach pain, epilepsy, vomiting, diarrhea, paralysis of the big toe and foot, cold feet, foot cramps, and abdominal tension. This point helps balance the yin aspect of the Great Regulator Channel. When energy flows well through SP 4, the body energy is balanced.

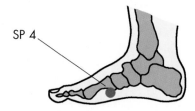

Fig. 5.11. The location of SP 4 (Spleen meridian)

KD 1 (Kidney Meridian)

Traditional Name: Yong Quan = Bubbling Spring

Location: In the hollow at the center of the ball of the foot when the toes are curled in; a sensitive spot (fig. 5.12).

Uses: To help calm the spirit. It opens the senses and connects the earth energy to the perineum.

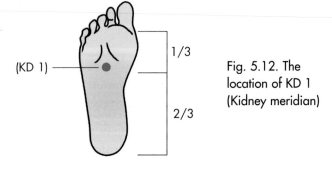

Fig. 5.12. The location of KD 1 (Kidney meridian)

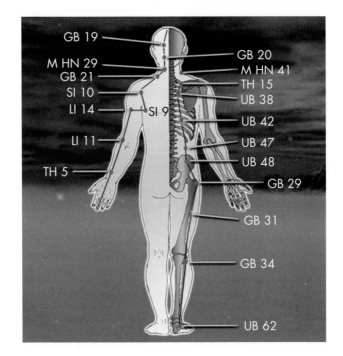

Fig. 5.13. The yang side of the body

The Entire Back (Yang) Route of the Channel: GB 41 to S 19

GB 41 (Gall Bladder Meridian)

Traditional Name: Lin Chi = Attending the Crying Child

Location: Facing the outside of the foot at the joint, in the upper space between the fourth and little toe (fig. 5.14).

Uses: To help to relieve arthritis, inflammation of the breast, hearing problems, ringing in the ears, irregular menstruation, insufficient breast milk, headaches, rheumatism, perspiration problems, and excessive water retention. This point helps balance the yang aspects of the Great Regulator Channel and the Belt Channel.

Fig. 5.14. The location of GB 41 (Gall Bladder meridian)

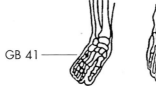

GB 41 ——

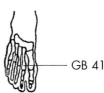

—— GB 41

UB 62 (Urinary Bladder Meridian)

Traditional Name: Shenmai = Extending Vessel

Location: On the outside of the ankle, in the small depression just under and slightly behind the ankle bone (fig. 5.15). Press straight into the side of the foot.

Uses: To relieve headache, mental confusion, epilepsy, dizziness, insomnia, backache, and aching of the lower extremities.

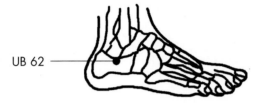

UB 62

Fig. 5.15. The location of UB 62 (Urinary Bladder meridian)

GB 34 (Gall Bladder Meridian)

Traditional Name: Yang Ling Chuan = Life Tomb Spring

Location: On the outside of the leg, in a hollow below the top of the fibula (slender, lower leg bone) (fig. 5.16).

Uses: To relieve rheumatism in the knees, weakness of the legs, pain or paralysis of the leg, soreness after exercise, headaches, abdominal problems, constipation, lower back tension, and extreme fright.

GB 31 (Gall Bladder Meridian)

Traditional Name: Feng Shih = Windy City

Location: Standing upright with the hands at the sides, the point is located behind the femur (thigh bone) where the middle finger touches the leg (fig. 5.16). The point is very sensitive to pressure.

Uses: To relieve paralysis of the legs and knee joint pain. Energy flowing through GB 31 encourages good energy flow to the knees, legs, hips, and back points.

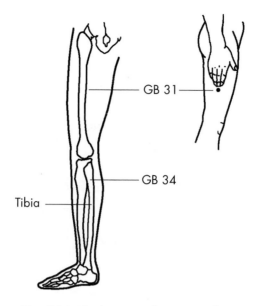

Fig. 5.16. The location of GB 31 and GB 34
(Gall Bladder meridian)

GB 29 (Gall Bladder Meridian)

Traditional Name: Chu Liao = Dwelling Bone

Location: At the joint of the top of the femur bone and the hip (fig. 5.17).

Uses: To relieve diseases of the hip joint and surroundings, and lower leg pain.

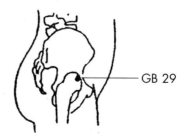

Fig. 5.17. The location of GB 29
(Gall Bladder meridian)

UB 48 (Urinary Bladder Meridian)

Traditional Name: Pai Huang = Round Tissue below the Diaphragm, Uterus, or Placenta

Location: Two fingers' width from the top of the sacrum (fig. 5.18). The point feels sore.

Uses: To relieve the pelvic area, abdominal problems, constipation, hemorrhoids, prostate gland, and urinary problems.

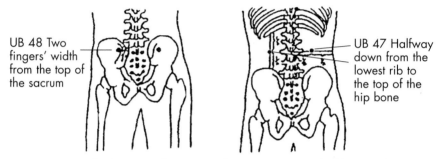

UB 48 Two fingers' width from the top of the sacrum

UB 47 Halfway down from the lowest rib to the top of the hip bone

Fig. 5.18. The location of UB 48 and UB 47 (Urinary Bladder meridian)

UB 47 (Urinary Bladder Meridian)

Traditional Name: Chi Shih = Room of Resolution

Location: On the back, halfway down from the lowest rib to the top of the hip bone, and halfway between the spine and the side of the body (fig. 5.18).

Uses: To relieve abdominal problems, appetite balance, genital problems, prostate, urinary, and kidney problems. Good energy flow through UB 47 strengthens the lower abdomen and releases energy flow to the lower back.

UB 42 (Urinary Bladder Meridian)

Traditional Name: Hun Men = Gate of the Soul

Location: On the back, between the ninth and tenth rib, and about two fingers' width below the bottom tip of the scapula (fig. 5.19).

Uses: To relieve stomach pain, liver problems, fullness in the chest, poor digestion, and fainting. Pressing this point releases the back and affects the diaphragm.

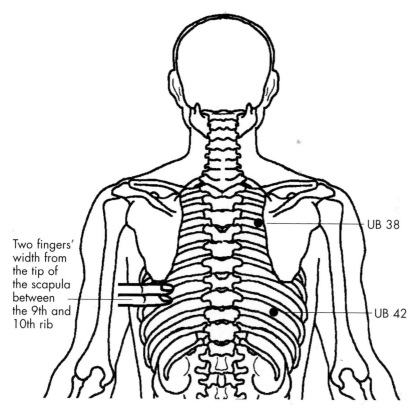

Two fingers' width from the tip of the scapula between the 9th and 10th rib

UB 38

UB 42

Fig. 5.19. The location of UB 42 and UB 38
(Urinary Bladder meridian)

UB 38 (Urinary Bladder Meridian)

Traditional Name: Kao Huang = Fat Tissue between Heart and Diaphragm

Location: On the back, between the fourth and fifth rib, between the spine and the right scapula (fig. 5.19). The point feels like a knot of muscular tension and is sensitive to pressure.

Uses: To relieve circulation and lung problems, release the neck, upper back, and arms, and to relieve respiratory difficulties, coughing, hyperactivity, and fatigue. Pressing this point strengthens the entire body. This is a very important point and can be used to treat many diseases.

TH 15 (Triple Heater Meridian)

Traditional Name: Tian Liao = Heaven's Seam

Location: Above the shoulder blade, toward the side of the neck (fig. 5.20).

Uses: To relieve pain in the scapula, back, neck, and the pain of fever.

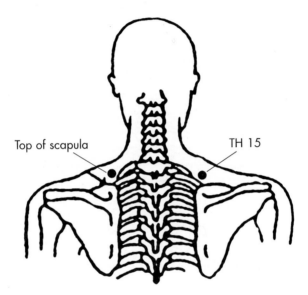

Top of scapula   TH 15

Fig. 5.20. The location of TH 15
(Triple Heater meridian)

SI 10 (Small Intestine Meridian)

Traditional Name: Nao Shu = Scapula Hollow (or Upper Arm Shu)

Location: On the back, on the scapula directly above the armpit and joint (fig. 5.21).

Uses: To relieve chills, fevers, inability to move the arm, soreness of the arm, hypertension, and shoulder pain.

SI 9 (Small Intestine Meridian)

Traditional Name: Jian Zhen = Shoulder Chastity

Location: On the back, just above the armpit (fig. 5.22).

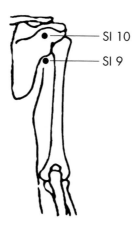

Fig. 5.21. The location of SI 10 and SI 9
(Small Intestine meridian)

Uses: To relieve shoulder problems, paralysis of the upper limbs, excessive perspiration in the armpits, pain in the shoulder blades, toothaches, deafness, and swelling of the joints.

The Yang Arm Route of the Channel: LI 14 to TH 5

LI 14 *(Large Intestine Meridian)*

Traditional Name: Binao = Arm and Scapula

Location: On the upper arm, above the midpoint between the shoulder and elbow (fig. 5.22).

Uses: To help clear vision, and relieve arm, shoulder, and eye problems.

Fig. 5.22. The location of LI 14 and LI 11 (Large Intestine meridian)

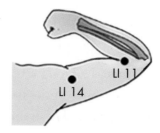

LI 11 (Large Intestine Meridian)

Traditional Name: Quchi = Crooked Pool

Location: At the front of the arm in the inner crease where the forearm joins the upper arm (fig. 5.22 on previous page).

Uses: To cool heat; can relieve arthritic pain in the arms, paralysis, hypertension, high fever, anemia, allergies, and skin problems.

TH 5 (Triple Heater Meridian)

Traditional Name: Waijuan = Outer Gate

Location: Two fingers' width above the wrist on the outside of the arm (fig. 5.23).

Uses: Helps to circulate stagnant chi; can relieve common colds, high fevers, pneumonia, deafness, insomnia, headache, stiff neck, and paralysis.

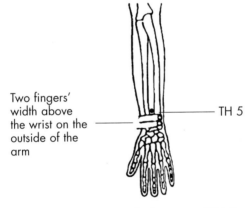

Two fingers' width above the wrist on the outside of the arm ——— ——— TH 5

Fig. 5.23. The location of TH 5
(Triple Heater meridian)

The Yin Arm Route of the Channel: PC 8 to LU 1

PC 8 (Pericardium Meridian)

Traditional Name: Laogong = Gakor's Palace

Location: At the center of the palm (fig. 5.24).

Uses: To cool the heart and drain heat, relieving heat exhaustion and chest pains.

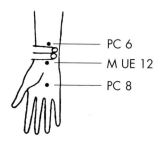

Fig. 5.24. The location of PC 8 and PC 6 (Pericardium meridian) and M UE 12 (Miscellaneous point)

M UE 12 (Miscellaneous Point)

Traditional Name: Nei Yangchi = Inner Yang's Pool
Location: At the center of the inner crease of the wrist (fig. 5.24).
Uses: To relieve paralysis and infantile convulsions.

PC 6 (Pericardium Meridian)

Traditional Name: Nei Guan = Inner Gate.
Location: Two fingers' width above the inner wrist (fig. 5.24).
Uses: To calm the heart and spirit and regulate chi; can relieve rheumatic heart disease, vomiting, chest pain, and stomachache.

PC 3 (Pericardium Meridian)

Traditional Name: Quze = Crooked Marsh
Location: On the middle of the crease of the inner elbow (fig. 5.25).
Uses: To open heart chi and disperse heat; can regulate the intestines, gastrointestinal problems, bronchitis, and heat exhaustion.

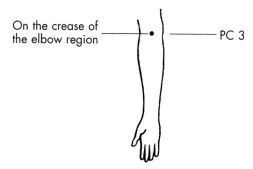

On the crease of the elbow region —— PC 3

Fig. 5.25. The location of PC 3
(Pericardium meridian)

PC 2 (Pericardium Meridian)

Traditional Name: Tianjuan = Heaven's Spring

Location: Next to the armpit in the front of the arm, within the biceps muscles (fig. 5.26).

Uses: To relieve cough, palpitations, and chest pain.

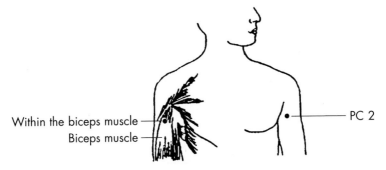

Fig. 5.26. The location of PC 2
(Pericardium meridian)

LU 1 (Lung Meridian)

Traditional Name: Zhong Fu = Central Radiance

Location: On the outside of the upper chest, below the clavicle (fig. 5.27).

Uses: To relieve bronchitis, pneumonia, asthma, tuberculosis, coughing, blocked throat, and congested nose.

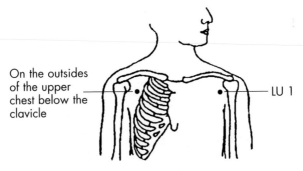

Fig. 5.27. The location of LU 1
(Lung meridian)

The Last Part of the Yang Back Channel: LI 16 to GB 19

LI 16 (Large Intestine Meridian)

Traditional Name: Fusu = Crest Bare

Location: In a hollow of the shoulder at the end of the clavicle (fig. 5.28).

Uses: To disperse blood congestion and relieve shoulder problems, convulsions, and neck problems.

GB 21 (Gall Bladder Meridian)

Traditional Name: Tian Jing = Shoulder Well

Location: On the shoulder, in a hollow of the collarbone near the neck (fig. 5.28).

Uses: To relieve uterine bleeding, back pain, and shoulder pain.

M HN 41 (Miscellaneous Point)

Traditional Name: Jingbi = Neck and Arm

Location: On the side of the neck, above the clavicle (fig. 5.28).

Uses: To relieve numbness in the arm and paralysis of the upper limbs.

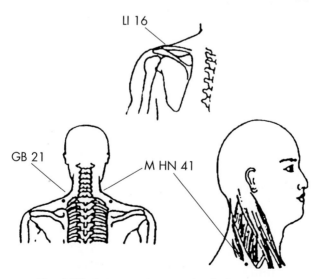

Fig. 5.28. Points on the yang back channel

M HN 29 (Muscle Point)

Traditional Name: Xinshi = New Recognition

Location: On the back of the neck between the third and fourth cervical vertebrae (fig. 5.29).

Uses: To relieve stiff neck, headaches, and sore throat.

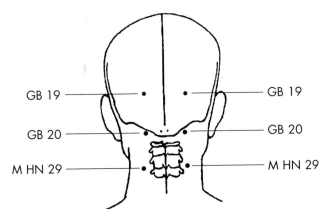

Fig. 5.29. Points on the back of the head and neck

GB 20 (Gall Bladder Meridian)

Traditional Name: Fengchi = Pool of Wind

Location: On the back of the neck in the hollow at the base of the skull (fig. 5.29).

Uses: To help a hot wind condition; can improve hearing and vision; can relieve the common cold, headache, stiff neck, hypertension, sinusitis, red eyes, deafness, and insomnia.

GB 19 (Gall Bladder Meridian)

Traditional Name: Nao Kong = Brain Hollow

Location: On the head and level with the upper border of the external occipital protruberance, directly above GB 20 (fig. 5.29).

Uses: To relieve muscle and coordination problems with the eyes from conditions such as MS, Parkinson's, and so on.

Opening the Great Bridge and Regulator Channels

There are two ways to open the Great Bridge and Regulator Channels: a short form in which you move your palm along the channels to feel the energy flow through them as a whole, and a long form in which you open each point along the channels individually. The long form provides the strongest sensation.

 ## Formula I (Short Form): Opening the Bridge and Regulator Channels as a Whole

This exercise enables you to feel a pure energy flow along the route of the channels without any blockages. To do this, you move the palm of your hand along the channel while feeling your third eye connect to each point. This will fill the route with a bright golden spiritual liquid, which will help to bring your mind into the pure energy body.

1. Start at the GB 17 points at the top of your head. Connect your palms with the points and feel the golden liquid drain in.

2. Now move your hands along the top of your head, connecting the energy to each point as you pull the liquid down past your third eye in a straight line through the front of your body.

3. Take the energy past the pelvic bones; on the inside of the legs the energy has a thick syrupy feel.

4. Take the energy into the Bubbling Spring points (KD 1).

5. Take the liquid up the outside of the legs and feel the golden liquid burn the toxins out of the hips.

6. Go up the spine slowly to the shoulders, then go around to the armpits, to the SI 9 points.

7. Use your right palm to pull the liquid along the outside of the left arm, then to the center palm point (PC 8), then pull it up the inside of the left arm to LI 16 on your left shoulder.

8. Switch the energy to the left hand to pull the energy from point SI 9 on the right arm to the center palm point of your right hand, then back up the inside or your right arm to LI 16 on your shoulder.

9. Using two hands, go up the neck and head to GB 17.

10. Take your palms along the points until you feel the path being cleared of toxins by the golden liquid chi. Do this several times until the path is soaked with energy.

Formula I (Long Form): Opening Each Point of the Bridge and Regulator Channels Individually

Preparation 1: Fusion of the Five Elements

The first preparatory step is to quickly practice Fusion of the Five Elements.

1. Either sit or stand, then smile down to your whole being.

2. Reactivate your pakuas, including the heart, facial, and universal pakuas. Feel these dynamic symbols spiral, purifying and stimulating your organs, five senses, and mind. Continue with this cleans-

ing of toxins until your organs, senses, and mind all feel as clear as crystals.

3. Then let the lower tan tien suck the refined energy into its center, to mix with its powerful energy and be more highly refined.
4. Take the multi-orgasmic compassion energy into each of the organs in the creation cycle to activate their divine energy again.
5. Then take these energies into the lower tan tien, and let them blend with this energy into a strong pearl.
6. Take the pearl to the perineum, and then through the Microcosmic Orbit several times until it has cleared a strong path. Let the pearl suck up the earth force, and the force of universal energy. Let the pearl go back to the perineum.

❂ Preparation 2: Opening the Thrusting Channels

The next step of preparation is to take the pearl into the three Thrusting Channels and slowly move it up and down to burn the toxins out of these channels.

1. Let your left arm hang down to the side with your fingers hanging down to the earth. Close your right nostril, and inhale as you pull up your left anus and suck the energy through the Left Thrusting Channel. Exhale and let all the toxic energy flow down the channel into the wanting, accepting earth.
2. Close both your nostrils, pull up the middle of your anus, suck the energy in through the Middle Thrusting Channel, and let the golden steam spread. Exhale down on the right side and let your right hand hang down to the side with your fingers hanging to the earth; keep your left nostril closed and let all the toxic energy flow down into the accepting earth.
3. Keep your left nostril closed, with your right arm hanging down, fingers hanging down to the earth. Inhale, pull up your right anus,

and suck the energy up through the Right Thrusting Channel. Let the pearl burn through the channel as you exhale and let all the toxins be sucked out by the accepting earth.

4. Repeat the procedure for the Middle Thrusting Channel, but this time, as you exhale down on the left side, keep your right nostril closed and your left arm hanging down to the earth.

5. Repeat steps 1 through 4 and then conclude with step 1.

6. Rest and feel the clean and open quality of the three Thrusting Channels and all the organs they penetrate. With your third eye you can still foster the energy flow up and down in the three channels. Feel the energy vitalize the Thrusting Channels.

◔ Beginning the Practice: Opening the Yang Points on the Head

1. Feel the pearl move through the Left and Right Thrusting Channels to point GB 16 on the Pai Hui (crown of the head). Press the Pai Hui with the middle fingers of both hands (fig. 6.1). This point is typically very sensitive to energy, so let the energy spiral deep. Then again press your fingers on the left and right sides of GB 16 until it feels numb and tingling.

Note: You do not have to get exactly on the point; just find the general area and notice where the energy seems to "click" into place. This place is also where you will get the strongest pulsation and therefore the best communication with the spot.

2. Keep both middle fingers on GB 16, and place your index fingers about an inch away on GB 17, and your ring fingers an inch away from the middle on GB 15 (see fig. 6.2 on page 76). Press and release these points a few times. Press them and move the skin in small circles, until you get a strong connection of tingling, energizing chi. Continue to press firmly on these points for some time.

Fig. 6.1. Left and Right Thrusting Channels

3. Then gently press the same three fingers on point GB 14 on both sides, in the middle of your forehead over your left and right eyes (see fig. 6.2 on page 76). When you have clicked with the points, pull the liquid chi from your crown to your forehead. Continue to press your fingers until you get a pulsating, tingling feeling of energy in your forehead.

Note: If you get tense or worried, GB 14 is probably blocked. Wrinkle up your brow, like when you are worried, and then release it to help the energy flow into your forehead. If you have stiffness in your face or neck, pressing GB 14 can help the energy activate and flow. These points are also very related to inner vision and consciousness, so activating a strong energy flow through them will help to clear your vision.

4. Now move the three fingers of both hands down to ST 2 on your cheekbones, in line with your pupils and GB 14. You may feel slight soreness here. Feel the energy draining in a line from your crown to your forehead, into your eyes and then to your cheekbone points, ST 2 (see fig. 6.2 on page 76).

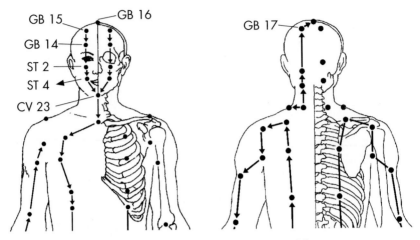

Fig. 6.2. Points to press on the head and face

5. Move your fingers to the ST 4 points at the corners of your mouth (fig. 6.2). Press in and slightly upward. You may feel soreness or tingling in your teeth due to the release of toxins. Drain the infinite chi energy from the crown into your eyes and the corners of your mouth.

6. Now release your hands and clasp them in the meditation position. Let the energy drain and flow throughout all these points on your head: GB 17, GB 16, GB 15, and the points down your face to ST 4.

7. Rest. Let the energy tingle and dance around in these points, blessing you. Feel the gratitude coming from these consciousness points and give thanks.

Opening the Points along the Front Routes, ST 4 to SP 4

1. Keep your fingers on ST 4 at the corners of your mouth and let the energy move to CV 23, as you use either thumb to press up into the chin toward your tongue. You may feel a little electrical charge as you press with your hand (fig. 6.3).

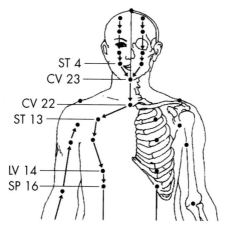

Fig. 6.3. Front routes

2. Use your left or right thumb to press into the top of your sternum toward the chest. Rest, then use your left index, middle, and ring fingers to gently press on CV 22 point above your sternum. Let the energy drain into this point, and relax; it may tingle. As you relax, connect the two points together and bring the energy down from your crown through the points on the face to your sternum.

3. Move the index, middle, and ring fingers of each hand from the points on your crown down to point ST 13 just under your collarbone. Massage this point with chi. Then move your fingers just above the nipples at ST 16. Let the divine energy flow from the crown slowly down to just above your nipples, and let it tingle and dance.

4. Place your right fingers and left fingers on ST 13 on each side. Then move your hands straight down to LV 14, between ribs eight and nine, on both sides. Feel the energy flow into these points. Massage these points until chi soaks deep into your bones; let the energy pulse deep into your fingers. Move the left and right fingers to just beneath your rib cage in line with your nipples, to point SP 16; let the Golden Elixir flow into it deeply.

5. Move your left and right fingers to SP 15 on both sides (fig. 6.4). Massage this energy in a spiraling chi motion. Also press into SP 13 on each side by your groin above your leg bones, in line with the above points. Feel the Golden Elixir flow, and let it move and dance deep into these points.

6. Move your fingers down to SP 10, just above your knee on each side. Feel the energy tingle and numb these points. Now move your fingers to SP 9 just below your knees, and let the elixir drain into these points, which will tingle and numb them as well.

7. Move your fingers to KD 6, one finger's width below your inner ankle on each side. Feel these points pulse and tingle. Move your hands to SP 4 on the inside of each foot, just under the ball of your foot. Let the energy tingle and numb these points when they connect to the points above.

8. Move your fingers to KD 1 (Bubbling Spring) on the bottom of each foot. This point is an antenna for earth energy, so open it wide while the elixir slowly flows in.

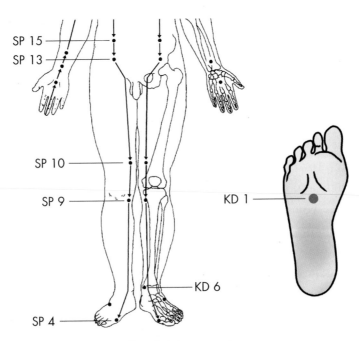

Fig. 6.4. Lower routes

9. Clasp your hands in the meditation position. Relax as the chi's spirit, the Golden Elixir, slowly drains from your crown to the soles of your feet.

10. Before you open your eyes, let the chi tingle and numb them. Open your eyes slowly and use the chi to see; it uses your consciousness, which is much easier on the eyes.

◑ *Moving the Energy along the Yang (Back) Route, KD 1 to SI 9*

1. As above, first put the three middle fingers of your right and left hands on GB 17, GB 16, and GB 15.

   Run the route again to ST 13.

2. Place your three fingers on ST 13 under the collarbone on both sides as before and hold them to press and circulate chi into the points. Repeat for each succeeding point down the front left side through ST 16 to KD 1 and GB 41 (see fig. 5.4).

3. Let the chi energy keep flowing up in one straight line on the outside of your ankles and legs from UB 62, through GB 34 and GB 31 into the hip, GB 29, to UB 48 on your back, a little above the top of the sacrum (see fig. 5.13).

4. Move the right and left hand fingers to your back points, UB 47, UB 42, and UB 38, all the way up to TH 15 at the top corner of your scapula.

5. Move the right and left hand fingers to the points SI 10 and SI 9, just above your armpits.

6. Clasp your hands in the meditation position. Let the energy slowly dance from the head to the soles of your feet up to SI 9 just above your armpits.

7. Before you open your eyes, let the energy numb and tingle them. Feel the steam build in your eyes as you slowly open them; connect your vision to the chi steam, which will make your vision looser and more relaxed. Give thanks as the chi elixir connects the points.

✪ Opening and Linking the Points of the Yang Arm Route (LI 14 to TH 5) to the Points of the Yin Arm Route (PC 8 to LI 1)

1. Put the three fingers of your right hand on point LI 14 on your left arm, then on LI 11, then on TH 5 above your outer wrist (fig. 6.5). Let the Golden Elixir slowly flow through these points.

2. Rest, close your eyes, and feel the energy drain through these points.

3. Then link the points on the outer (yang) side of your left arm to the inner (yin) side, beginning with moving your right fingers to point PC 8 on your left palm (fig. 6.6).

4. Then move your fingers up along the inside (yin) of your left arm through points M UE 12, PC 6, PC 3, PC 2, and LU 1.

5. Rest and feel the elixir moving through your yang and yin routes on the left arm. Feel your pores open and your blood generating electricity.

6. Then, using your left hand, repeat steps 1 through 5 on your right arm to activate the chi elixir, open your pores, and generate electricity.

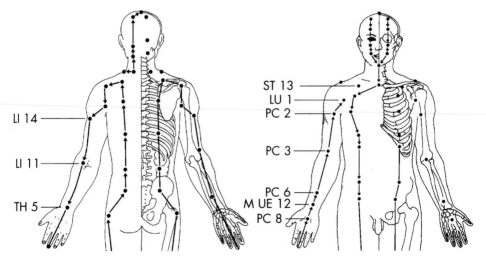

Fig. 6.5. The yang arm route

Fig. 6.6. The yin arm route

⊙ *Opening the Upper Part of Both Yang Channels to Connect the Right and Left Sides*

1. Move the fingers of both hands from LU 1 to LI 16 on both of your shoulders at the same time (fig. 6.7).
2. From there go to GB 21, M HN 29, and GB 20 at the base of your skull.

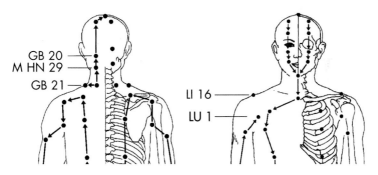

Fig. 6.7. The upper yang route

3. Put your hands in the meditation posture, feel the energy slowly dance through the left and right sides of the Great Bridge and Regulator Channels. Link the two sides together by moving the elixir in the mind.

Daily Practice: A Quick Morning Checkup of the Eight Psychic Channels

This quick checkup incorporates elements of the base Fusion practices found in *Fusion of the Five Elements* and *Cosmic Fusion*, where a full explanation of the terms and practices referred to can be found.

1. Smile down on your being, quickly form your divine pearl, and bring it down into your perineum. Let the pearl flow though the Microcosmic Orbit 6 times.
2. Now return the pearl to the perineum, and clear the three Thrusting Channels, including the leg routes.

3. Women: guide your energy into the accepting earth, then absorb the energy and spiral it deeply inward, clockwise and then counterclockwise. Start the Belt Channel (the protective Belt Route that surrounds the Thrusting Channels) spiraling around the core of your being, up to and above your crown. Spiral it counterclockwise and powerfully absorb the heavenly force into your crown and body. Spiral the Belt Channel clockwise down deep into the earth and accept the divine earth force. Repeat, spiraling your Belt Channel counterclockwise slowly up to your crown and then back to the earth again in a clockwise direction.

4. Men and women: split your energy pearl at your feet and begin the flow of energy through the Great Bridge and Regulator Channels from the inside of your left and right feet (SP 4). Run the energy up the front of the channels into your groin and all the way up the front side of your body to GB 14 on your head. Let the energy stream up to your crown, passing into GB 15, GB 16, and GB 17, then down into LI 16. As you stream the energy up the inside of your legs and the front of your body, you will feel energy flow along the outside of your legs and the back of your body at the same time (most of your yin and yang points are located just opposite of each other). From LI 16 take the energy to LU 1, then along the inside of the arms to PC 8; from there take it over to TH 5 on the outside of the arms and back up to LI 16. From there let the elixir stream up to the crown (GB 16) again.

Energy Protection and Forming the Energy Body

The formulas in this chapter help you cultivate and strengthen the clear pure energy necessary to the formation of an energy body. When you have completed these practices, you will be ready to move on to the more advanced practices of Taoist Inner Alchemy.

Formula II:
Spinal Cord Cutting from the Throat

1. If you are starting fresh, always start with Fusion of the Five Elements to form a dynamic pearl, then circulate it deeply in your Microcosmic Orbit for a few rounds.
2. Hold the pearl at the throat center at the top of the sternum, and drill the cosmic energy into the center until it starts to feel numb. Inhale, exhale, and project the pearl out from the throat. Orbit it around the outside of your head to the back and continue the orbit so that the pearl penetrates or "cuts" through your body to C7 (see fig. 7.1 on page 84). Bring the pearl through C7 and project it out through the front of your body. Continue orbiting

Project the pearl out of your throat, go around your head, and cut through your vertebrae.

Fig. 7.1. Spinal cord cutting

the pearl in progressively larger loops so that it cuts through each of your cervical, thoracic, and lumbar vertebrae, in turn. Once they are numb and tingling, slowly continue with the orbiting of the pearl down through your sacrum and coccyx.

3. Finish by orbiting the pearl in progressively smaller loops back up to your throat.

 ## Formula III:
Spinal Cord Microcosmic Orbit

This exercise enables you to send chi energy deep into your spine. Use it to pack chi deeply into your spine until it begins tingle and you get a pleasurable numb feeling. This will release previously locked spinal chemicals into your brain (fig. 7.2). When you pack the chi deep in your spine it will easily feel as good as a child's, with strength

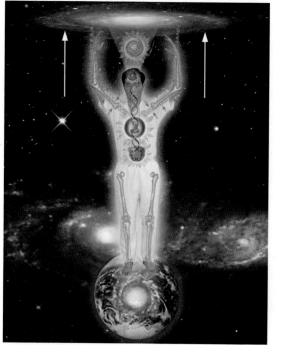
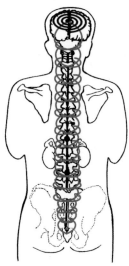

Spinal cord
Microcosmic Orbit

Fig. 7.2. Packing chi in the spine will release
precious chemicals into the brain.

and sensitivity that are rarely experienced. Instead of feeling cramped, your spine will be able to release precious hormones into the brain. It is also necessary to pack the chi deep to protect it when your spirit body enters the Mid-Plane between the earthly plane and the cosmos in the higher practices. If you lack energy when you enter the Mid-Plane, you will lose your foundation and sensitivity, which will cause you to lose focus.

1. Practice your Fusion of the Five Elements meditation and move the Golden Elixir of your pearl through your Microcosmic Orbit. Tighten your anus as you let the pearl swim into your sacrum. Then allow it to slowly swim up the inside of the back of your spinal cord until it "burns" its precious energy into your Jade Pillow at the base of the skull. Then bring the pearl slowly

into your brain (fig. 7.3). Feel how the elixir has changed after it has mingled its energy with the spine. Continuing on in the brain, wrap the pearl around your frontal lobe inside the skull. Then slowly return the pearl down the inside of the front of your spinal column, so that it encircles the whole length of the spine (fig. 7.4).

2. Let the pearl swim into the coccyx and through it, then up the outside of the back of the spinal cord. Slowly wrap it around your frontal lobe and then let it swim down along the outside of the front of your spinal cord; return the elixir slowly into your coccyx.

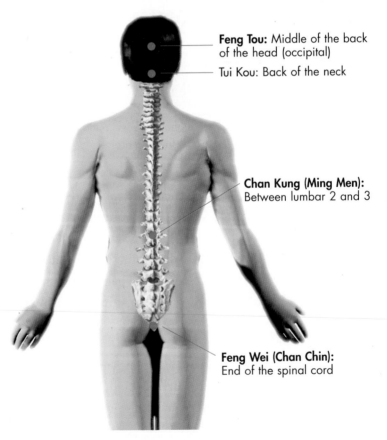

Feng Tou: Middle of the back of the head (occipital)

Tui Kou: Back of the neck

Chan Kung (Ming Men): Between lumbar 2 and 3

Feng Wei (Chan Chin): End of the spinal cord

Fig. 7.3. Golden Elixir on the inside of the back of the spine

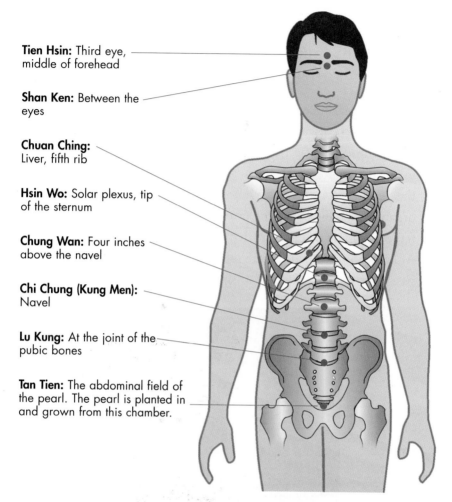

Tien Hsin: Third eye, middle of forehead

Shan Ken: Between the eyes

Chuan Ching: Liver, fifth rib

Hsin Wo: Solar plexus, tip of the sternum

Chung Wan: Four inches above the navel

Chi Chung (Kung Men): Navel

Lu Kung: At the joint of the pubic bones

Tan Tien: The abdominal field of the pearl. The pearl is planted in and grown from this chamber.

Fig. 7.4. Golden Elixir on the inside of the front of the spine

3. Swim the pearl around your coccyx. Spiral it up around the outside of the spinal cord deep into the space of your brain. Spiral the pearl around your skull, then spiral it down on the inside of the spinal cord to the coccyx. Let it rest there as it steams, tingles, and numbs this spot.

4. Let the pearl steam and spiral around in your spinal cord Microcosmic Orbit a few times until the spinal cord is dripping and tingling with chi.

Formula IV: Protecting your Spine, Organs, and Glands with Cutting from the Third Eye

1. Hold the pearl deep within your third eye, and feel it steam, then project the pearl out and orbit it clockwise or counterclockwise down through your neck. Orbit it in progressively larger loops to cut through your thoracic and lumbar vertebrae (fig. 7.5). Cut the pearl deep into your whole body, driving it deep into all your organs and glands. Cut the pearl back into the third eye and again feel your spine dripping with energy from the core.

2. After lodging your pearl in your third eye, drain the energy down past your throat and chest to spiral it in your lower tan tien.

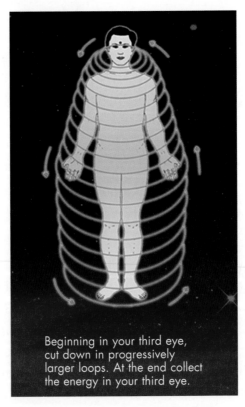

Beginning in your third eye, cut down in progressively larger loops. At the end collect the energy in your third eye.

Fig. 7.5. Cutting from the third eye

Formula V: Drilling your Head with Energy

This exercise is used to spiral energy deep into your head so you are sensitive enough to receive the higher energy frequencies. Powerfully drill your head to raise your spiritual tan tien to the next level (fig. 7.6). Drilling will help to clear the brain and give it a cool, fresh, tingly feeling. As your brain is the most important organ of your body, drilling the chi deeply into it will lead to outstanding benefits.

1. Drill your head with energy by spiraling the pearl from your third eye to the back of your head. Repeat by drilling horizontally from points on your forehead to the back. Continue to deeply spiral energy all over your face and head, at obvious as well as not so obvious points. You must be very thorough to open the head to higher frequencies. Drill deep into your eyes until they are tingling and numb. Drill the energy deep into your nose and ears. Drill the Golden Elixir through your face and temples; move it from front to back and side to side through your brain.

2. Vertically drill the pearl down through your Pai Hui. Drill the energy all over your crown, again in both obvious places and not so obvious places. Feel the brain being permeated with multi-orgasmic energy; the feeling, of course, is beautiful.

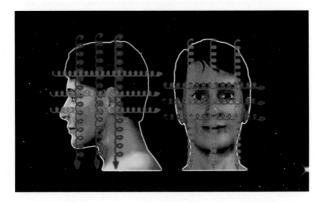

Fig. 7.6. Compared to a stagnated head, a head
sensitized in chi is more receptive to higher vibrations.

Formula VI: Cutting the Senses

The Tao allows you to communicate with parts of your body that you may never have thought to work with. Cutting the energy of the pearl into your senses releases stagnated chi and activates new chi. Each of your senses has its own spirit that you can "intimately" touch if that is your desire. Unblocking the stagnant energy enables you to reach the higher consciousness of your senses, which enhances the work with the energy or chi body described later in this chapter. Our senses are our ways of communicating with the external world, and the chi body will be of much higher vibration and realization if you have gained enough energy in your senses so that, for example, you are seeing with the vision of chi and smelling with the focused power of chi. When you open your senses up to this level they will have infinite potential, and a new light of life will shine, which is a beautiful thing (fig. 7.7).

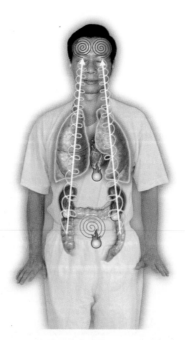

Fig. 7.7. Empowering the five senses
with chi opens new doors and is very
important for your energy body.

To start, hold the pearl about half an inch in front of your eyes, then spiral it in three figure-eight motions in the following manner, starting from the third eye (fig. 7.8).

1. Slowly spiral the pearl down to the bottom of the left eye, letting the pearl drive through your skin as if making a ditch. Circle the pearl to the top of your left ear. Then bring it down the back of your left ear to the bottom, digging it through like a ditch. Then circle it up to your left eyebrow.

2. Bring the pearl across your third eye and cut it down to the bottom of your right eye, then up to the top of your right ear. Circle around the back of your ear, cutting up to your right eyebrow, and join the first spiral deep in your third eye.

3. From your third eye spiral the pearl down to the left side of your nose, and dig down to the right corner of your mouth in a half circle. Spiral under your mouth to the left corner of your mouth, then cut the pearl across to the right side of your nose. Return it to your third eye.

4. When you are finished, collect and spiral the energy deep into your third eye.

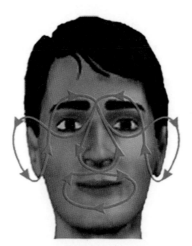

Fig. 7.8. Drill the energy deep into your senses to
stimulate a new interesting communication.

Formula VII: Butterfly Protection of Your Body

In the butterfly protection exercise you spiral energy around your whole body. This exercise is used in the martial arts to prevent an opponent from being able to find the center of your energy and attack you. It makes your energy feel strong and thick from every angle so an opponent cannot find a way in. In the higher practices we use this exercise for the same reason: to hide our center of energy so nobody can "attack" us. It provides very good psychic protection. It can prevent those with "negative" energy from even noticing your radiant energy, so it protects you from their jealousy or any inclination they may have to abuse your energy (fig. 7.9).

1. Start at ST 16 just above your nipples. (This point is slightly higher on women than on men.)
2. Spiral your pearl in line with the body from ST 16. As it spirals, direct it to cut slowly through your rib cage on both sides of your body in outward and downward arcs, like the wings of a butterfly, and then cut back in. The right spirals should move in a clockwise direction and the left in a counterclockwise direction.
3. Your spirals should get larger every time until they slowly include your whole body. Then slowly expand the spiraling out from your body into your aura. As the energy spirals slowly in your aura, feel a

Fig. 7.9. Increase the spirals to slowly encompass your body, then spiral out into your aura.

Golden Elixir connection deep in your energy field, until the whole field feels like an expansion of your heart's energy. Make 20 spirals.

4. Collect the energy at your navel, then do Chi Self-Massage.

 ## Formula VIII: Sealing the Aura

This Taoist practice serves to sensitize your being to your aura, seal your aura to preserve energy, and create a thicker aura to broaden the pleasurable sensitivity of your body and protect your being.

1. Begin with spiraling the pearl deep into your navel, then slowly send the pearl of energy down the front of your right leg to the big toe of your right foot, then across to the big toe of your left foot (fig. 7.10).

2. Run a sheet of energy across each toe of your left foot and up the outside of your left leg. Continue up the outer left side of your body to your armpit. Then trace the inside of your left arm, thumb, and fingers. Trace the outside of your left arm, over your left shoulder, then over your crown.

3. Now trace down the outside of your right arm and fingers, then up the inside of the arm. Trace down the right side of your body, along the outside of your leg to your toes. Trace each toe and bring the sheet of energy up the inside of your right leg, around

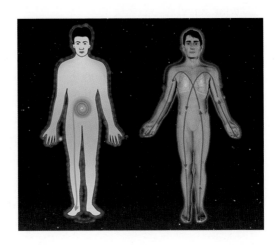

Fig. 7.10. Circulate your pearl through these routes until they are all sensitive.

your perineum, to the inner left leg, down to your left toes. If you wish to do only this part of the exercise, jump the energy to your right big toe and repeat the full procedure, but this time in reverse, starting with tracing your right toes and then going up the outside of your right leg. To finish the procedure, bring the energy up and collect it at your navel. If you wish to continue to the next part of the exercise, do not jump the energy back to the right toes and instead move on to the following steps.

4. Trace the front side of your left leg up to your left pelvis. Cross the energy over your solar plexus to your right collarbone, down the inside of your right arm to your fingers. Trace up the outside of your right arm and bring the energy up over your crown. Continue down the outside of your left arm and fingers, then up the inside of your left arm to your left collarbone. From there, bring the energy down the front side of your body, crossing over the solar plexus again, to your right hip, and then down the front side of your right leg.

5. Bring the energy up the back side of your right leg, then cross over T11 (the eleventh thoracic vertebrae) to the left scapula (fig. 7.11). Trace down the inside of your left arm, around the fingers, up the outside of the left arm, over the crown, down the outside of your right arm, up the inside of your right arm to your right scapula and across T11 to go down the back of your left leg to end at the toes. Bring the energy up the front of your left leg and collect it at your navel.

6. Rest. Turn your senses and mind inward. Empty your mind in your tan tien. Feel the presence of your aura around you with a density like that of water. Feel that the water is massaging your spirit with many minute but strong hands. Experience your aura like a dense golden or blue fog that easily penetrates your body as if you were not an object but only a spirit. Feel your spirit implode with multi-orgasmic and compassion energy (fig. 7.12).

7. Multiply this energy; let it implode until you are on the brink of tears and beyond. Slowly dance inside this energy and feel the potential that the human race would have if the whole world were

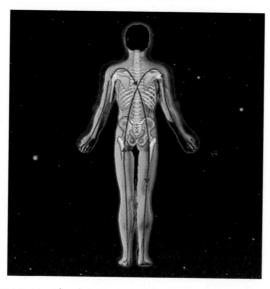

Fig. 7.11. Your back is as important to sensitize as the front.

Fig. 7.12.
Feel your aura
massaging your
spirit. Feel your
spirit implode with
multi-orgasmic
and compassion
energy.

educated to live in this energy, rather than how it is educated by the contemporary education system. Now you have a strong connection to your aura. Finish with Chi Self-Massage.

Forming the Energy Body

Your capacity to form the energy body builds upon the high sensitivity cultivated by all of the previous practices such as forming the pakuas. All of the practices in this chapter are important, but mixing compassion energy with multi-orgasmic energy may be the most crucial. You have to have an intense "electric" sensation in order to have a powerful experience in the energy body. Once you have practiced to this level, you are ready to form the pearl into an energy body by transferring the energy of the Microcosmic Orbit, Thrusting Channels, Belt Route, and the Great Regulator and Bridge Channels from the physical body to the energy body above (fig. 7.13).

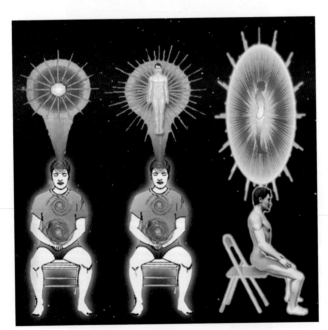

Fig. 7.13. Feel the pearl implode in multi-orgasmic and compassion energy, giving more power to you.

Extend the Microcosmic Orbit.

Extend the Thrusting Channel.

Extend the Belt Route into the body above.

1. Always begin with Fusion of the Five Elements to clear out your negative emotions.
2. Condense the pearl and circulate it in the creation cycle, Thrusting Channels, and Belt Channel.
3. Run the pearl through the Microcosmic Orbit and control its movement with your senses.
4. Move the pearl to the perineum. Inhale the life force in short sips, drawing in 10 percent of your lungs' capacity, and pull up your anus. Inhale up to your navel, then inhale the life force up to your heart.
5. Inhale up to the crown. Swallow your saliva (imagine swallowing upward) and exhale forcefully to open the crown and shoot the pearl out into the surrounding cosmos.
6. Feel the universal force, the forces of the North Star and Big Dipper above your head, and the cosmic particle force in front of you as they shine into your pearl (fig. 7.14). Feel your pearl start to absorb this energy, then feel this energy expand like a Big Bang or multi-orgasmic implosion.

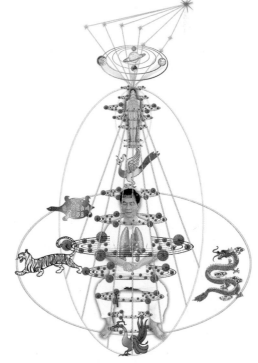

Fig. 7.14. Feel the pearl absorbing the energies of the Big Dipper and cosmos.

7. Bring your awareness to your feet. Feel the earth energy flow up through your feet to supply your energy body. Your pearl will continue to expand with all the energy coming to it from outside your physical body.

8. Relax your senses as you form the energy body above your crown. Count the years of your age as your energy body grows. This will help you to remember that your energy body has always been with you. Form the energy body in whatever way most benefits you, such as with radiant skin.

9. Run the Microcosmic Orbit in your physical body. Open your crown and slowly transfer the pathway of your Microcosmic Orbit into your energy body.

10. Form another sensitive pearl in your cauldron, and shoot the pearl into your energy body. Circulate the pearl through both of the Microcosmic Orbits.

11. Move your Thrusting Channels into your energy body.

12. Circulate energy throughout your Belt Channel, spiraling it up through your crown to encircle your energy body (fig. 7.15). Feel the Belt Channel spiral around both your physical body and your energy body, connecting all the channels in both bodies and protecting them. Do this until your energy body is numb and tingly and electricity easily sparks throughout both bodies, particularly in the spiritual chakras in your head.

13. Continue to practice until you are in full control of your energy body, with multi-orgasmic energy easily permeating it. Slowly and gently bring your awareness to this body, letting it travel carefully bit by bit, while remaining closely connected with your physical body (especially with the cauldron in the tan tien) and the earth. Let it collect and absorb the energies of the North Star and Big Dipper, the planets, and other stars.

14. When you are ready, shrink your energy body to a pearl. Activate the cranial pump. Press your tongue up, clench your teeth, pull your chin back, pull up your anus, and look up to your crown. Feel the beating in your heart and the pulse at your crown.

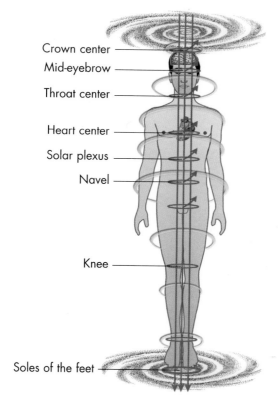

Crown center
Mid-eyebrow
Throat center
Heart center
Solar plexus
Navel
Knee
Soles of the feet

Fig. 7.15. Circulate energy throughout the Belt Channel around your whole being.

15. Activate the lead light (the guiding light that you can feel shining out through your crown), and let it shine upward. It may feel like a crown. Draw the pearl down into the lead light. Inhale and draw the pearl back into your crown to energize it.

16. Move the pearl in the Microcosmic Orbit and nourish the physical body with all the energies the pearl has absorbed. Then bring it down to the navel and to the cauldron at the body's center. Collect, spiral, and condense the energy in the cauldron.

17. Sit back and turn the focus of your awareness in toward your center. Rest and stay in this energy. Finish with Chi Self-Massage

Note: The energy that the pearl/energy body absorbs nourishes your physical body as well as your energy body and the spirit body formed in the practices of the Immortal Tao.

Summary

When you have become more familiar with the practices offered in this book, you will reach a point where you don't need to follow explicit directions for every step of each exercise. Referring to the practice summaries offered here should be enough to remind you of the steps for each practice.

 ## Opening the Great Regulator and Great Bridge Channels

After you have opened all the points of the Great Bridge and Great Regulator Channels you can use this summary to go through the points more quickly. However, you still should make sure that all of the points are fully sensitized or you will not gain the full benefits of the practice. You will know when they are sensitive enough because the practice will then be fun and very pleasurable.

1. Seat yourself in the proper position and do the Inner Smile to all of your organs. Also do Fusion of the Five Elements and Cosmic Fusion thoroughly.
2. Stream your pearl into your perineum. Split it into two pearls: inhale them up through your Right and Left Thrusting Channels to the middle and side Crown points (GB 16). Take your time,

because the spine will always provide additional chi as they move upward.

3. Stream the pearls to the GB 17 points (at the rear top of your head), back to GB 16, then to the GB 15 points (at the front top of your head), then stream them down to the GB 14 points just above your eyebrows.

4. Stream the pearls down to the ST 2 points below your eyes, then to the ST 4 points above your lips.

5. Stream both pearls under your chin to CV 23 then to CV 22 at the bottom of the throat.

6. Cut just below the collarbone on both sides to ST 13 and then ST 16 at the ribs, to LT 14 (lower ribs), then to the abdomen point SP 16 (spleen), on to SP 15 and SP 13.

7. Stream your pearls to SP 10 and SP 9, above and below your knees.

8. Go to the inside of your heels to the KD 6 points and inside your lower feet to the SP 4 points.

9. Go underneath your feet to KD 1 (Bubbling Spring) points and to GB 41 points on the outside of your feet.

10. Stream the pearls under the outside of both ankles to UB 62, to GB 34 on the outside of your legs below the knees, to GB 31 on the outside of your thighs, to the inside of your hip joints at GB 29, and the inside of your hip bones at UB 48.

11. Then take them up your back on both sides to UB 47, UB 42, UB 38, and TH 15 (upper scapula), then back to UB 42.

12. Stream your pearls up on both sides to SI 10, then down to SI 9 and down the outside of your arms to LI 14 and LI 11.

13. On both arms, stream the pearls to TH 5 on the back of your wrists, then to PC 8 on your palms, then up your inner arm to PC 3 on the inside of your elbow, then to PC 2 in your arm near your armpit, to LU 1 just below your clavicle near your armpit.

14. Then take them to your shoulder points, LI 16, up the neck points (GB 21, M HN 41, and M HN 29), to your Jade Pillow, then to the back of the skull points, GB 20 and GB 19. Finally, connect with the Crown points.

15. Do the entire cycle with breathing 9 times, feeling the energy elixir movement opening up all your meridians.
16. Collect the new energy at your navel. Now do Chi Self-Massage.

 ## Opening the Five Senses by Cutting

1. Move your pearl to your third eye, then move the pearl in three figure eights around your sense openings.
2. From your third eye, go below your right eye to the top of your right ear, around the back to the bottom of your right ear, up to your right eyebrow and return to your third eye; then go under your left eye to the top of your left ear, around the back to the bottom of the ear, then up to your left eyebrow and back to your third eye.
3. From there, go down the left side of your nose, then under your nose to the right side of your mouth, under your mouth to the left side, across to the right side of your nose and up to your third eye.
4. Repeat all three figure eights 3 times.

 ## Heart Center Cutting with a Butterfly Motion to Protect Your Aura

1. Stream your pearl to the heart collection point in your sternum.
2. Split it into two pearls and spiral them around your nipples, cutting through the heart center in outward and downward arcs like butterfly wings. The right spiral should move in a clockwise direction and the left should move counterclockwise.
3. The spirals should grow larger each time, until they reach deep into your body's aura.
4. Repeat 20 times.
5. Collect the energy at your navel, then do Chi Self-Massage.

 ## Sealing Your Aura

1. Refine the pearl in your cauldron by spinning the first four pakuas,

then move the pearl down the inside of your right leg to the right big toe.

2. Jump the pearl to your left big toe. Spread it to trace the left toes, stream it up the outside of your left leg, up your left side past the ribs to the left armpit and down the inside of your left arm and fingers. From your left fingers take it up the outside of your left arm over your left shoulder and up over your crown.

3. Stream the pearl down to your right shoulder, then along the outside of your right arm to your fingers, then up the inside of your right arm. Now take it down your right side along the outside of your right leg, down to your toes. Trace your toes, then stream the pearl up the inside of your right leg around your genitals, down your inner left leg to the big toe.

4. Jump the pearl to your right big toe and repeat the full procedure, but this time in reverse, starting with tracing your right toes and then going up the outside of your right leg.

5. After completing the cycle and returning the pearl to your right big toe, jump it to your left big toe. Then move the pearl to trace the front side of your left leg up to your left pelvis, then across your solar plexus to your right collarbone. Move the pearl down the inside of your right arm and fingers, then up the outside of your right arm and over your crown. Continue down the outside of your left arm and fingers to the inside of your left arm and up to the left collarbone. Then take it down your chest across your solar plexus and abdomen to the right hip and down the front of your right leg.

6. Trace the pearl up the back side of your right leg to your right buttocks. Go across to your left scapula and down the inside of your left arm. Take the pearl around to your left hand, up the outside of your left arm and over your crown. Then drain the energy down the outside of your right arm, up the right inner arm to your right scapula. Take the pearl across to your left buttocks down your left back leg to the left toes. Stream the pearl up the front of your left leg to your left hip and then to your navel.

7. Collect your new energy at your navel and do Chi Self-Massage.

Forming the Energy Body

1. Follow all of the Fusion formulas given in chapters 6 and 7 (Formula I through VIII) and conclude with streaming the pearl to your perineum.
2. Inhale in sips up to the navel, then to your heart and crown. Swallow your saliva on your exhale, open your crown, and shoot the pearl out into the cosmos.
3. Relax your senses as you expand the pearl into your energy body above your crown.
4. Form another pearl and run it through the physical body's Microcosmic Orbit. Then circulate the pearl in the Microcosmic Orbit of both your physical body and your energy body.
5. Project the psychic channels into your energy body.
6. Thoroughly practice all eight Fusion formulas in your energy body.
7. Gather and shrink your energy body into a pearl and draw it into your physical body.
8. Collect the energy at your navel and do Chi Self-Massage.

CONCLUDING REMARKS

The ultimate goal of all of the Fusion practices given in *Fusion of the Five Elements, Cosmic Fusion,* and this book is that of preparing your being for the Immortal Tao practices. It is very important that your energy is prepared to handle the larger vibrations that you will experience. Your energy sensitivity needs to be cultivated until you can move energy anywhere in your body and drill your compassion energy and your multi-orgasmic energy deep into a given point. If you have done this all over your body, you will know that you are ready for the higher Immortal Tao practices. You will experience a very obvious change in your energy, as the purest energies will be running through your body, mind, and spirit. If you have not yet attained this, you can achieve it by going through the Fusion practices more slowly and thoroughly.

When you are ready for the Immortal Tao practices you will feel a deep love for life, a love that is overflowing. You will feel your spirit attempting to jump out of your body in pure happiness and glee. It will make you want to show those around you what is possible; you will not want to just keep the energy to yourself. You will be energized by the possibility of creating something significant that cannot be destroyed by all the troubles of the world. You may have a vision sparking in your third eye. When the energy starts taking you, you will no longer belong to your mind. You will belong to the universe. When that happens you will naturally flow into the Immortal Tao practices offered by the Universal Tao.

The key question you need to answer is what you want from life. Your answer is important because you will receive much stronger energy if your mind is turned toward the life force in a very effective manner. Of course you have to be humble and ask Heaven to bestow the energy upon you that will enable you to brighten this Earth. It is very important to want the energy to heal yourself so you can brighten the world. To see the true essence of the energy, you have to make this your only dream. If you think about it, this is realistically all that you need: a healthy body to create the same in the world. A nice house and things like cool spiritual artwork or nice jewelry are just add-ons.

This path is that of recognizing your true nature, understanding who you really are. If you do understand, you will see that you are a channel for the divine energy to shine through. We are all the same in this respect: we all want to be healthy and want the world to be happy. If we consider the idea of the universe giving us free will, we see that we have the choice to use chi to heal our personal body and world body, or we have the choice to do anything else, but all other choices are of the material world. Chi energy is the substance of the spiritual realm: the energy that can heal anything, providing consciousness is in the right place. This is so because chi is infinite, and there are infinite possibilities within it. You need to cultivate your sensitivity to the chi, while having a humble mind toward it so you can reap the rewards. Then you will naturally develop your powerful energy body and your spiritual body.

 # Bibliography

Chia, Mantak. *Advanced Chi Nei Tsang: Enhancing Chi Energy in the Vital Organs.* Rochester, Vt.: Destiny Books, 2009.

———. *Bone Marrow Nei Kung: Taoist Techniques for Rejuvenating the Blood and Bone.* Rochester, Vt.: Destiny Books, 2006.

———. *Chi Nei Tsang: Chi Massage for the Vital Organs.* Rochester, Vt.: Destiny Books, 2007.

———. *Cosmic Fusion: The Inner Alchemy of the Eight Forces.* Rochester, Vt.: Destiny Books, 2007.

———. *Energy Balance through the Tao: Exercises for Cultivating Yin Energy.* Rochester, Vt.: Destiny Books, 2005.

———. *Fusion of the Five Elements: Meditations for Transforming Negative Emotions.* Rochester, Vt.: Destiny Books, 2007.

———. *Golden Elixir Chi Kung.* Rochester, Vt.: Destiny Books, 2005.

———. *Healing Light of the Tao: Foundational Practices to Awaken Chi Energy.* Rochester, Vt.: Destiny Books, 2008.

———. *Taoist Cosmic Healing: Chi Kung Color Healing Principles for Detoxification and Rejuvenation.* Rochester, Vt.: Destiny Books, 2003.

About the Author

Mantak Chia has been studying the Taoist approach to life since childhood. His mastery of this ancient knowledge, enhanced by his study of other disciplines, has resulted in the development of the Universal Tao System, which is now being taught throughout the world.

Mantak Chia was born in Thailand to Chinese parents in 1944. When he was six years old, he learned from Buddhist monks how to sit and "still the mind." While in grammar school he learned traditional Thai boxing, and soon went on to acquire considerable skill in Aikido, Yoga, and Tai Chi. His studies of the Taoist way of life began in earnest when he was a student in Hong Kong, ultimately leading to his mastery of a wide variety of esoteric disciplines, with the guidance of several masters, including Master I Yun, Master Meugi, Master Cheng Yao Lun, and Master Pan Yu. To better understand the mechanisms behind healing energy, he also studied Western anatomy and medical sciences.

Master Chia has taught his system of healing and energizing practices to tens of thousands of students and trained more than two thousand instructors and practitioners throughout the world. He has established centers for Taoist study and training in many countries around the globe. In June 1990 he was honored by the International Congress of Chinese Medicine and Qi Gong (Chi Kung), which named him the Qi Gong Master of the Year.

The Universal Tao System and Training Center

THE UNIVERSAL TAO SYSTEM

The ultimate goal of Taoist practice is to transcend physical boundaries through the development of the soul and the spirit within the human. That is also the guiding principle behind the Universal Tao, a practical system of self-development that enables individuals to complete the harmonious evolution of their physical, mental, and spiritual bodies. Through a series of ancient Chinese meditative and internal energy exercises, the practitioner learns to increase physical energy, release tension, improve health, practice self-defense, and gain the ability to heal him- or herself and others. In the process of creating a solid foundation of health and well-being in the physical body, the practitioner also creates the basis for developing his or her spiritual potential by learning to tap into the natural energies of the sun, moon, earth, stars, and other environmental forces.

The Universal Tao practices are derived from ancient techniques rooted in the processes of nature. They have been gathered and integrated into a coherent, accessible system for well-being that works directly with the life force, or chi, that flows through the meridian system of the body.

Master Chia has spent years developing and perfecting techniques for teaching these traditional practices to students around the world through ongoing classes, workshops, private instruction, and healing sessions, as well as books and video and audio products. Further information can be obtained at www.universal-tao.com.

THE UNIVERSAL TAO TRAINING CENTER

The Tao Garden Resort and Training Center in northern Thailand is the home of Master Chia and serves as the worldwide headquarters for Universal Tao activities. This integrated wellness, holistic health, and training center is situated on eighty acres surrounded by the beautiful Himalayan foothills near the historic walled city of Chiang Mai. The serene setting includes flower and herb gardens ideal for meditation, open-air pavilions for practicing Chi Kung, and a health and fitness spa.

The center offers classes year-round, as well as summer and winter retreats. It can accommodate two hundred students, and group leasing can be arranged. For information worldwide on courses, books, products, and other resources, see below.

RESOURCES

Universal Healing Tao Center
274 Moo 7, Luang Nua, Doi Saket, Chiang Mai, 50220 Thailand
Tel: (66)(53) 495-596 Fax: (66)(53) 495-852
E-mail: universaltao@universal-tao.com
Web site: www.universal-tao.com

For information on retreats and the health spa, contact:
Tao Garden Health Spa & Resort
E-mail: info@tao-garden.com, taogarden@hotmail.com
Web site: www.tao-garden.com

Good Chi • Good Heart • Good Intention

 Index

Page numbers in *italics* refer to illustrations.

BOOKS OF RELATED INTEREST

Fusion of the Five Elements
Meditations for Transforming Negative Emotions
by Mantak Chia

Cosmic Fusion
The Inner Alchemy of the Eight Forces
by Mantak Chia

Tan Tien Chi Kung
Foundational Exercises for Empty Force and Perineum Power
by Mantak Chia

Chi Nei Tsang
Chi Massage for the Vital Organs
by Mantak Chia

Chi Self-Massage
The Taoist Way of Rejuvenation
by Mantak Chia

Healing Light of the Tao
Foundational Practices to Awaken Chi Energy
by Mantak Chia

The Taoist Soul Body
Harnessing the Power of Kan and Li
by Mantak Chia

Wisdom Chi Kung
Practices for Enlivening the Brain with Chi Energy
by Mantak Chia

INNER TRADITIONS • BEAR & COMPANY
P.O. Box 388
Rochester, VT 05767
1-800-246-8648
www.InnerTraditions.com

Or contact your local bookseller